The Villista Prisoners
of
1916-17

James W

Yucca Tree Press

First Printing   September 2000

Hurst, James W.
    THE VILLISTA PRISONERS OF 1916-17
        1. Columbus, New Mexico—Pancho Villa Raid.   2. New Mexico—
        History.   3. Villa, Francisco.   4. Pershing Punitive Expedition into
        Mexico, 1916.   5. United States - Army - History - Pershing Punitive
        Expedition into Mexico, 1916.
        I. James W. Hurst.   II. Title.

Library of Congress Catalog Number: 00-104710
ISBN: 1-881325-44-X

To Annabelle, Paula, Jonathan and Max

Acknowledgments

Thanks are due to Lee Goodwin, past Senior Archivist, Daphne S. O. Arnaiz-DeLeon, Senior Archivist, and the staff of the State Records Center and Archives, Santa Fe. The staff of the Luna County Clerk's Office, Deming was most helpful in my search for indictments and records associated with the Villistas. Velia Miranda, Clerk, Sixth Judicial District Court, Silver City took time from her busy schedule to help me look for records of Villista Guadalupe Chavez. The staff of the Deming Museum Archives, Deming provided access to several interesting newspaper accounts of the raid and subsequent trials. Peter "Piñon" Crum, Reference Librarian of the Public Library at Silver City, was most helpful with local history files and the Grant County Death Records. Professor Louis R. Sadler, History Department, New Mexico State University, was kind enough to read the manuscript. His comments and suggestions were beneficial to both the structure and content of what follows. John J. Slonaker, Chief, Historical Reference Branch of the US Military History Institute provided the photocopy of General Pershing's "Report of the Punitive Expedition." Mitchell Yockelson, Archivist, Old Military and Civil Records Access Programs of the National Archives was instrumental in finding the "Records of Prisoners Book" in the Punitive Expedition's Intelligence Files. Fernando Lucero of La Mesa, New Mexico provided photos from his personal collection for consideration and use. Special thanks to Jonathan D. Hurst, who read the entire trial transcript and offered invaluable comments and observations. Any errors are, of course, mine.

James W. Hurst
Mesilla, New Mexico

Table of Contents

List of Illustrations

Preface

My interest in Francisco Villa's March 9, 1916 raid on Columbus, New Mexico began several years ago with a visit to Columbus, to Pancho Villa State Park, and to the Visitors' Center at old Camp Furlong. I had virtually no knowledge of the raid itself, or of the Punitive Expedition that was to follow. My ideas of the affair, such as they were, had probably been conditioned by novels and films to the extent that they had little connection to the subtleties of historical reality. Columbus had been attacked by Mexican bandits, buildings were burned, looting occurred, citizens were killed, the bandits were driven away by soldiers stationed nearby, prisoners were taken, a trial of sorts was held, and public hangings followed: that now seems to me to have been the extent of my knowledge.

Within my limited outlook the bandits themselves were probably a rabble of ignorant, illiterate conscripts motivated by a mixture of fear of their leader and a lust for loot; the trial would have been a Judge Roy Bean west-of-the-Pecos fiasco; and the hangings nothing more than legal lynching. A story, in short, worthy of many of the literary stereotypes of the old "Wild" West and of the images of the Silver Screen which had been so much a staple of my childhood entertainment. As I began a study of the raid and its aftermath, however, a somewhat different picture emerged.

The journey that has produced this book began with an essay written by Professors Charles H. Harris III and Louis R. Sadler, historians at New Mexico State University. Their reference to a transcript of the trial of six captured Villistas sent me on the first of several trips to Santa Fe, New Mexico and the State Records

Center and Archives. This transcript is the only known record of the Villista trials still in existence, and it offers us an unfiltered look into the courtroom: the judge, the attorneys, the jurors, the witnesses, and the defendants all emerge from the past and speak directly to us. It was during the reading and study of this one hundred and eighty-four-page transcript that the different picture mentioned above began to develop.

Quotations taken from the trial transcript are given exactly as they appear in the original, and notations are added only when necessary for the reader's understanding. Periods and question marks were seldom placed at the end of a sentence in the original document, and I have added them where necessary. The use of the editorial *sic* has been kept to a minimum and is used only where, in my judgment, it is necessary for the reader's understanding. Since I am not an attorney and have no expertise in matters of the law, the trial transcript was sent to one who has the necessary knowledge and experience. Jonathan D. Hurst, JD, Assistant State's Attorney for Morgan County, Illinois generously offered his time to read the trial transcript and to suggest answers to my questions. His comments will be found in the Commentary following the text, and the reader's attention is directed to them in several footnotes.

As Judge Edward L. Medler was preparing for the trial of the six Villistas who would be tried together, questions of fairness arose. In the course of the narrative, the reader will see Judge Medler's reaction to suggestions that the defendants could not receive a fair trial in his courtroom. I believe that Judge Medler's assurances of a fair trial for the accused Villistas were correct. Whatever mistakes in preparation for the trial the attorney for the defense, Buel R. Wood, might have made (see Trial Commentary), they cannot be blamed on Judge Medler. His instructions to the jury were meticulous and fair: twenty-six separate instructions took fifteen pages in the trial transcript.

Governor Octaviano A. Larrazolo's position expressed in his *Executive Order* of November 22, 1920 that the prisoners held in Santa Fe as a result of General Pershing's Punitive Expedition were all private soldiers pressed into service in Villa's "army" against their will, and ignorant of the expedition's purpose, is simply not supported by the evidence. The intelligence data gathered by

Lieutenant Nathan Campanole, Intelligence Officer for the Punitive Expedition, indicates that ten of the twenty-two prisoners held in the Stockade at Colonia Dublan were officers. All prisoners admitted their involvement in the Columbus raid with two exceptions: Pilar Gomez, a civilian, who was subsequently released, and Enrique Adame who was with Villa's forces but due to illness was forced out of the line of march and never got to Columbus.[1] Further evidence indicates that Villa informed his troops of his intentions on several occasions.

Of the twenty-two men held in the stockade at Colonia Dublan, Mexico, eight turned themselves over to, or were arrested by, Captain José Maria Espinoza of the Namiquipa Home Guard. The others were captured and arrested by officers and men of the Punitive Expedition, often with the aid of civilians and other prisoners (Villista Lt. Juan Muñoz was, with others, most helpful). In addition to Gomez, five other suspected Villistas were questioned and released. The Columbus raiders brought back to the United States by the Punitive Expedition to be turned over to civil authority in New Mexico had been carefully and fairly interrogated, and their treatment was as humane as possible given the circumstances.

In the narrative that follows, my hope is that I have come close to the guidelines for the historian's craft expressed in the prayer of Thomas Aquinas: "Give me sharpness in understanding, sagacity in interpretation, facility in learning, and abundant grace in expression."

James W. Hurst
Mesilla, New Mexico

---

[1] See Appendix J

Villa's most recent biographer, Friedrich Katz, believes Villa's primary reason for the attack on Columbus was his "... firm belief that President Woodrow Wilson had concluded an agreement with Carranza that would virtually convert Mexico into a U.S. protectorate." Cf. 67, fn. 265.

Courtesy: Poe Family Photograph Collection,
State Records Center and Archives, Santa Fe, New Mexico.

Introduction

In the early morning hours of March 9, 1916, Francisco Villa attacked the border town of Columbus, New Mexico with a force of four hundred and eighty-five men. In a matter of hours the Villista raiders were in retreat, pursued by hastily assembled units of the 13th Cavalry led by Major Frank Tompkins.[1] With the return of Tompkins' command of fifty-six mounted cavalrymen and four officers, the Columbus affair was over. In his report to Colonel Herbert J. Slocum, Tompkins described "..having been gone seven and one half hours, covered 25 to 30 miles of rough country, fought four separate rear guard actions without the loss of a single man, and inflicted a loss of from 75 to 100 killed ... ."[2] The raid, the burning,[3] the looting, the killing, and the pursuit covered probably no more than nine hours; yet over eighty years later the Columbus raid continues to fascinate both students and scholars of the Mexican Revolution. Two American scholars have suggested that the "... definitive history of the Columbus raid has yet to be written."[4]

Mexican writers have shown themselves to be skeptical in regard to Tompkins' report. Frederico Cervantes asserts that the Villista losses reported by Tompkins were not retreating Villistas, but were Mexican inhabitants of Columbus who had fled in fear of Army reprisals. Cervantes also claims that the owners possibly set the fires in the commercial buildings in Columbus themselves in order to take advantage of the situation and collect the insurance.[5] Victor Ceja Reyes asserts that the 13th Cavalry was beaten by Villa's attack and fled in confusion. Tompkins' account was an exaggerated one, made in order to redeem the Army's reputation and make heroes of the 13th Cavalry.[6]

Scholarly debate has centered in large part around Villa's motivation: what was his reason for the attack? There is not now, and probably never will be, a conclusive answer to the question. The major theses advanced by scholars are summarized by Professors Harris and Sadler,[7] and while the arguments over Villa's reason

1

Wounded Bandits at Columbus, N.M.

Of the five wounded Villistas taken during the raid, Elias
Morras (standing with head bandaged) died in Deming
(March 19, 1916). On the cot in the foreground is Juan Sanchez
(hanged June 9, 1916); second and third cots, unknown
(died of wounds); fourth cot, Jesus Paiz, the boy who lost
a leg as a result of a wound.
To the left of the tent pole is Captain Ryan, 13th Cavalry.
Courtesy: Charles Poe Photo Collection (#62649),
State Archives and Records Center, Santa Fe, New Mexico.

for attacking Columbus continue, one element of the story is mired in confusion: the fortune and number of the Villista prisoners. The following examples may serve to illustrate the nature and extent of the confusion.

Lieutenant John P. Lucas, 13th Cavalry, in the fight at Columbus from the beginning, wrote: "We were also criticized for taking so few prisoners. We did take, I believe, five wounded men and they were, I understand, later tried and hanged for murder."[8]

In *Strong Man of the Revolution*, Larry Harris wrote: "The eighteen Villista prisoners were taken to Deming. Nine of them were subsequently hanged and the other nine were hurried off to prison in Santa Fe."[9] In the introduction to Harris' book, Andrew Gulliford of Middle Tennessee State University wrote: "Fifteen Mexicans taken prisoner were tried by jury and hanged in Deming, New Mexico."[10]

Haldeen Braady wrote: "Military officials succeeded in holding from the irate citizens thirteen Villista prisoners in their custody, these being shortly conveyed for their protection to Deming, New Mexico. A trial of sorts occurred there nearly three months later, and two of the guilty marauders met death by hanging."[11]

James A. Sandos, using the Pershing Papers, reported that "Ninety of his [Villa's] followers were killed and seven captured."[12] Sandos wrote that sixteen more raiders were captured by the Punitive Expedition and were tried and imprisoned, but were later pardoned by New Mexico Governor Octaviano Larrazolo who contended that the men were merely following orders and therefore not subject to American jurisprudence.[13]

The following pages attempt to clarify, as best as the existing evidence will allow, who the prisoners were, and what price they paid for their involvement in the raid on Columbus.

---

[1] Colonel Frank Tompkins, *Chasing Villa: The Last Campaign of the U.S. Cavalry* (Silver City, New Mexico: High Lonesome Books, 1996), 56. Tompkins' force consisted of fifty-six mounted cavalrymen and four officers.

[2] *Ibid.*, 57.

[3] According to Cervantes, the Villistas asserted that the fires in the commercial buildings were possibly set by the owners themselves in order to take advantage of the situation and collect the insurance. *Ibid.* See Appendix M.

[4] Charles H. Harris III and Louis R. Sadler, *The Border and the Revolution: Clandestine Activities of the Mexican Revolution: 1910-1920* (Silver City, New Mexico: High Lonesome Books, 1990), 109.

[5] Frederico Cervantes, *Francisco Villa y La Revolución* (Ediciones Alonso, Mexico 1, D.F., 1960), 538. See Appendix M.

[6] Victor Ceya Reyes, *Yo, Francisco Villa y Columbus* (Centro Librero La Prensa, S.A. de C.V., 1987), 121. See Appendix L.

[7] *Ibid.* In addition see E. B. White, "The Muddied Waters of Columbus New Mexico," *The Americas* 32:1 (July 1975), 72-98; F. Katz, "Pancho Villa and the Attack on Columbus, New Mexico," *The American Historical Review* 83:1 (February 1978), 101-30; J. A. Sandos in "Communications," *The American Historical Review* 84:1 (February 1979), 304-06; and F. Katz, *Ibid.*, 306-07.

[8] Tompkins, *op.cit.*, 53.

[9] Larry Harris, *Strong Man of the Revolution* (Silver City, New Mexico: High Lonesome Press, 1995) 2nd printing, 92.

[10] *Ibid.*, ix.

[11] Haldeen Braady, *Cock of the Walk: The Legend of Pancho Villa* (Albuquerque, New Mexico: University of New Mexico Press, 1955), 133-34.

[12] James A. Sandos, "German Involvement in Northern Mexico, 1915-1916: A New Look at the Columbus Raid," *Hispanic American Historical Review* L:1 (February 1970), 81, *fn.* 84.

[13] *Ibid., fn.* 85.

Columbus, New Mexico.
*Courtesy: Poe Family Photograph Collection, New Mexico
State Records Center and Archives, Santa Fe, New Mexico.*

Chapter 1
The Columbus Seven
The First Trial

The earliest indictment found in the County Clerk's Office in the Luna County Court House at Deming, New Mexico was Cause (Case) #651.[1] On April 14, 1916 an indictment handed down by the grand jury charged Juan Sanchez, Pablo Sanchez, and Jesus Paiz with the murder of J.J. Moore.[2] In subsequent indictments, the three men were charged with the murders of Charles D. Miller,[3] James T. Dean, and Paul Simon. In four indictments, the grand jury charged Francisco Villa with murder in the deaths of Simon, Dean, Moore, and Miller. The grand jury continued its work with the indictments of Eusevio Renteria, Taurino Garcia, José Rodriguez, Francisco Alvares, José Rangel, and Juan Castillo. They were indicted jointly for the murders of Dean, Simon, Moore, and Miller. In addition to Cause #666, mentioned above, the grand jury concluded its session with the indictment of Pablo Sanchez for murder in the death of Miller. Of all the above indictments, it would be #652 and #664 that would send six Villistas to the gallows for murder.

Unfortunately, few of the documents of the *State of New Mexico vs. Juan Sanchez*, #652, District Court of Luna County, survive. The judge's instructions to the jury, the jury's verdict, the death warrant, the list of witnesses, and the sheriff's certification of the hanging are all that remain of the trial documents. In his instructions to the jury, Judge Edward L. Medler[4] indicated that the defendant's plea of not guilty placed upon the State the burden of proof beyond a reasonable doubt of the material allegations in the indictment. He continued: "Included in the indictment are Pablo Sanchez and Jesus Pias, charged with the same offense jointly with the defendant upon trial, but these two parties Pablo Sanchez and Jesus Pias, are not now on trial and as to them you will have no concern in reaching a verdict."[5] On April 24, 1916, the jury returned a verdict of guilty of murder in the first degree as charged in the second count of the indictment, and José Sanchez was sentenced to be "… hung by the neck until dead … ." on May 19, 1916.[6]

---

[1] The Luna County Clerk's Office (hereinafter LCCO) holds no records of the Villista trials. The records held are microfiche copies of incictments, warrants, execution orders, witness lists, verifications of executions and, in one case, expense records.

[2] J.J. Moore was a merchant.

[3] Charles D. Miller was an engineer for the State of New Mexico; James T. Dean was a grocer and merchant in Columbus; Paul Simon was a Corporal in the 13th Cavalry Band.

[4] Edward L. Medler was Judge of the Third Judicial District of the State of New Mexico sitting and acting in the District Court of Luna County in the place of Colin Neblitt, Judge of the Sixth Judicial District, by authority of Clarence J. Roberts, Chief Justice of the State of New Mexico. Cause #652, LCCO. The Third Judicial District is Doña Ana county; the Sixth Judicial District is Grant, Hidalgo, and Luna counties.

[5] Cause #652, LCCO. There is no indication in the surviving documents of the reasons for excluding Sanchez and Piaz from trial. Jesus Piaz was a boy of twelve who came to Columbus with his father Captain Piaz, an aide to Francisco Villa. While looking for his father in the confusion of the raid, Jesus was wounded in the left leg, The wound was so severe that the boy's leg was amputated (Santa Fe *New Mexican*, March 23, 1916. Although indicted, he was not prosecuted and appeared as a witness before Albert B. Fall's Senate Subcommittee on Foreign Relations, then meeting in El Paso, Texas. While apparently no trial record for Pablo Sanchez exists, he is listed as prisoner 560 CJ in the *New Mexico Federal Prisoner Roster 1913-1952* (State Records Center and Archives, Santa Fe, New Mexico).

[6] *Ibid.*

The stockade at Columbus, New Mexico,
where the Villa prisoners were first kept.
Courtesy: Poe Family Photo Collection,
State Records and Archives, Santa Fe, New Mexico.

Chapter 2
The Second Trial

The *State of New Mexico vs. Eusevio Renteria et al.,* Luna District Court Case #664, 1916, is the only trial transcript extant.[1] There is nothing in the trial transcript that explains why the defendants were tried for the murder of Charles D. Miller, rather than for the murders of Dean, Simon, or Moore. The decision to try the defendants for the murder of Miller may have stemmed from the circumstances of his death, and the fact that he was well known and respected throughout the state. He was shot and killed in front of the hotel which was the center of the violent action during the raid, thus making it easier for the State to convince a jury of the validity of the prosecution's strategy of *accomplice liability* (Trial Commentary #6). Miller was a graduate of New Mexico College of Agriculture and Mechanic Arts as a civil engineer and was Assistant Territorial Engineer from 1907-1910 and Territorial Engineer from 1910-1912. He was active in Republican politics, Treasurer of the Young Men's Republican Club of Santa Fe, and a thirty-second degree Scottish Rite Mason. He was the brother of J.O. Miller, Cashier of the First National Bank of Las Cruces and a cousin of J.A. Miller of Miller & Craig law firm of Albuquerque.[2] The State of New Mexico was represented by its Assistant District Attorney, J.S. Vaught; the defendants were represented by Attorney Buel R. Wood.

Before the trial began, Judge Medler had received several protests. The protests came in the form of telegrams and a telephone call. The telegrams were delivered to Medler in his court by Special Agent E.B. Stone of the Bureau of Investigation. The first telegram came from the Attorney General of the United States, the second from General Frederick Funston, Commanding General of the Southern Department, San Antonio, Texas, and the third from the U. S. Secretary of State Robert Lansing. Each telegram protested the trial of the Villistas "…on the ground that it would involve the United States in international complications with

The Columbus Seven.
The men are numbered from back row left to right. #1 was not
tried. #4 is the jailor, Archer. #2 Juan Sanchez; #3 José Rodriguez;
#5 Eusevio Renteria; #6 Francisco Alvarez; #7 José Rangel; #8
Taurino Garcia; #9 Juan Castillo. Identifications were made
through comparisons to penitentiary inmate photos and are judg-
ments on the part of the author. #3, José Rodriguez is a certainty.
Courtesy: Charles Poe Photo Collection,
State Archives and Record Center, Santa Fe, New Mexico.

Mexico."[3] When asked what his decision was regarding the telegrams, Judge Medler replied:

> I told Mr. Stone that the defendants were regularly indicted by a properly impaneled grand jury of Luna County; that they were in charge of the Sheriff of Luna County; that the grand jury had previously reported that the jail in Luna County was insanitary and not a proper place to confine prisoners; and that to continue the trial in this case would involve their being held in jail for six months, and I could see no reason why the court could not proceed to try this case on the following morning; that General Pershing was in Mexico ... trying to arrest Francisco Villa, a co-defendant named in this Indictment; and that if the trial of these raiders would involve the United States in international complications, to my mind it would seem that the United States was already involved.[4]

Judge Medler then spoke by telephone to Summers Burkhart, the United States Attorney at Albuquerque. Burkhart said he had instructions to go to Deming and protest the trial on the ground that the defendants could not receive a fair trial. The protest, Burkhart said, was not a negative reflection upon the court, but rather a belief that given the nature of public feeling in the area, a fair trial was not possible. Judge Medler "...assured him that as far as [he] had anything to do with it as judge of the court that they would have a fair trial ... ."[5]

Jury selection went smoothly and quickly, with only one challenge for cause. F.C. Parish, a New Mexico resident for two and one-half years and engaged in general merchandising, stated he could not sentence a man to death. Judge Medler explained to him that the jury did not sentence, it returned a verdict. Mr. Parish responded by saying that he could not vote guilty if he knew that a guilty verdict meant death for a defendant. The Court sustained the prosecution's challenge, and Parish was excused.[6] The jury was made up of seven farmers, a cigar dealer, a livery stable manager, a stock handler, a machinist, and an automotive livery manager.[7] The Court asked Attorney Wood if he wanted the witnesses put under the rule, and he replied that he did not.[8] With the jury seated and sworn, the judge directed the State to begin its case.[9]

13

J.S. Vaught began the State's case:

> Gentlemen of the Jury: The State in this case expects to
> prove to you that on the morning of the 9th of March,
> 1916, one Charles D. Miller was killed at Columbus, and
> we expect to prove to you by the admissions made by
> these six defendants that on the said 9th day of March,
> 1916, that these six defendants and each of them were
> in Columbus and were assisting in the perpetration of a
> felony at that time and that this showing will be made by
> the statements that were made by these six defendants.
> We do not expect to show you that either of these
> defendants fired the shot that killed Charles D. Miller,
> or that they were close by the place where Charles D.
> Miller was killed but at the time that he was killed they
> were in the immediate vicinity assisting in the commis-
> sion of a felony.[10]

Following his brief statement, the prosecutor called his first
witness, T.A. Hulsey, Deputy Sheriff, Columbus, New Mexico.[11]

Deputy Hulsey testified that he was home on the morning of
March 9, 1916, and about 4:24 a.m. Mexicans entered the town
shooting , and the firing lasted until about 6:00 or 6:25 a.m. He
drew a sketch of the area under attack and explained to the Court
where the raiders were in relation to various landmarks: "I seen
them all around. They were everywhere, and seemed to be of a
common will. There were three officers; they had on leggins [sic]
and two buglers and one on each side of them."[12] Hulsey ran from
his house and jumped into a large hole in his back yard from which,
he testified, he saw raiders firing their rifles from in back of the Fix
It Shop. He went on to testify that Charles D. Miller came out of
the hotel, attempted to start his automobile, and fell back and lay
motionless on the ground.[13] Hulsey testified he saw looting from
the Lemmon and Rumbley store and watched as the raiders
retreated in a southwesterly direction across the railroad track.

When asked if he had seen the defendants before, Hulsey
replied that he had seen them last on April 13, 1916 at the Army
hospital in Columbus. He had seen Francisco Alvares several months
earlier making adobes in Columbus. He had seen Taurino Garcia at
the Hilario Ochoa ranch in February, when he had accompanied

14

Sheriff Stephens to the ranch to recover a stolen saddle. The defense attorney objected twice to Hulsey's testimony regarding seeing the men earlier and was twice overruled.[14] Hulsey recalled his conversations with the prisoners in the Army hospital tent. They told him that Villa was present with the raiders to the international border; that the officers led their own groups to the town; and that they were holding horses outside of town during the raid.

Under cross-examination, the witness said the raiders yelled "Viva Mexico, Viva Madera, Viva Villa!" Attorney Wood asked: "… you cannot state, can you, on your oath that you identify and recognize as actual participators in the looting and raiding any of these defendants?" Hulsey answered, "No."[15] The hour of noon had arrived and the Court took adjournment until 2:00 P.M. The jury was placed under the charge of the bailiffs and were cautioned about speaking to anyone regarding the case.

The second witness called by the State was L.A. Riggs, Deputy U.S. Collector of Customs, Columbus, New Mexico. Riggs testified he was in his bedroom at the Custom House when at about 4:30 A.M. shooting and yelling broke out. He left the house with his wife and babies as soon as it was possible, and together they made their way to the military hospital. They worked with the wounded, and at about 6:30 A.M. he left for the telegraph office.

Q. [J.S. Vaught]: ""Did you see any of the parties who were doing this shooting— any of the raiders there on this morning?"

A. "No sir."

Q. "Did you see any of them?"

A. "No sir, not until after they were dead or wounded."[16]

Asked if he saw a body in front of the Commercial Hotel, Riggs replied that he saw a body he was told was that of Charles D. Miller. The defense attorney objected and was overruled by the Court. When asked if he had ever seen the defendants before, Riggs replied that he had seen them at the Army hospital in Columbus on April 13, 1916 (a defense objection was overruled). The witness stated he neither offered a reward nor made any threats to get the defendants to talk. Each defendant said that he was with Villa.

During cross-examination, Attorney Wood asked: "You never seen [sic] any of these defendants personally involved in the raid?"

Riggs answered, "No sir[.]" and continued his testimony by saying that the defendants simply told him "… that they had been there."[17]

B.S. Aguierre, line rider for the Customs Service, Columbus, New Mexico was the third witness called by the defense. He testified that he was in the Commercial Hotel at the time of the raid and was awakened about 4:40 A.M. by shots and shouting. The noise he heard was coming from the direction of Lemmon and Rumbley's store. He stated that he was in the hallway when he saw Villistas, who had broken into the hotel, coming up the stairs. He ran to the back of the hotel, got out through a window, and ran east to a nearby adobe house. From there he could see the smoke and fire coming from Lemmon and Rumbley's store. At daybreak, he made his way to the Army camp and by this time the Villistas were in retreat toward the west edge of town. He saw no recognizable individuals, but only groups of men he identified as Mexicans.

Asked by the State if he has seen any one, or all, of the defendants prior to the trial, Aguierre replied that he had seen them all in the Army hospital at Columbus and had questioned them regarding their presence at Columbus at the time of the raid. Each defendant admitted, according to Aguierre's testimony, that he was there at the time of the raid. José Rodriguez claimed that he was a Carranzista captured by Villa and forced to come with the raiders. Aguierre identified Taurino Garcia as present at the ranch of Hilario Ochoa two months before the raid when Ochoa's house was searched for guns and ammunition. The witness concluded his testimony for the State by stating that he neither threatened nor offered a reward for the defendants' statements.

During cross-examination, Aguierre was asked: "During all the time that you were there [in Columbus during the raid] and observed these things you didn't see any of the defendants?" He replied: "No. I might have seen them but I don't recognize them."[18] In response to the organization and orderliness of the Villista, Aguierre replied that he did not observe any organization or orderliness to the raiders.

The State's fourth witness was P.K. Lemmon, Jr. He testified that he was home the morning of the raid, having come home from Hachita on the train about 3:00 A.M. He heard shooting and thought the Army was having some sort of sham battle until he heard shouting in Spanish: "Viva Villa; Viva Mexico; mator las gringoes."[19] Lemmon stated that he heard a password passing from one side of the raiders to the other: "Mexico ... ." The defense attorney objected that the testimony about a password was irrelevant, it was a conclusion on the part of the witness, and it had no bearing on the murder which was what the trial was about. The objection was overruled. Lemmon testified that he did not recognize any of the raiders he saw, and he did not see any military uniforms on men. When asked by the Court how many men he saw that morning, he replied that he had seen between three and four hundred.

The attorney for the State asked Lemmon if he had seen the defendants prior to the trial, and he replied that he had seen them the night of April 13, 1916 at the Army hospital in Columbus. While there he talked only to Eusevia Renteria, who admitted he was in town and asserted the other defendants were in Columbus as well. According to Lemmon, Renteria said Villa was with the raiders. When Lemmon asked Renteria why the raiders did not attack the morning train, he was told that the raiders were too late for the train. The defense objected:

> I don't like to make objections but if these defendants are going to incriminate themselves to the extent of being guilty of other crimes, than this, we simply have to call for a trial on these other charges. The evidence shows that all these defendants admit to coming into Columbus on the morning of March 9th and coming back out of Old Mexico in company with United States soldiers in a wounded condition. That is the evidence which the State is using to [missing word?]these defendants with xxx physical participation with the raid on Columbus and any other statements made outside of that is irrelevant and cannot be part of the res gestae.[20]

Court: "Did he [Renteria] talk about the train that went through Columbus?"
Lemmon: "Yes sir."
Court: "Overruled!"
Defense: "Exception!"

Lemmon stated that Renteria claimed to know nothing of Villa's plans and had nothing to do with the looting and burning. Under cross-examination, Lemmon stated that from what he observed the Villistas were bandits, not soldiers. He stated that he did not see any of the defendants during the time of the raid.[21]

The fifth and final witness for the State was Lurid Fillmore, an Army Hospital Corpsman with twenty-three years' service. He first saw the defendants on April 11, 1916, when they were brought to the Columbus hospital between six and seven o'clock in the evening. Fillmore stated that he had seen Francisco Alvares at the Gabilando Ranch the previous October. Alvares tried to escape from the hospital, Fillmore testified, but was caught and returned. Asked by the State if the prisoners discussed the Columbus raid, Fillmore replied:

> Well, they didn't go so far into the details because they didn't seem to understand anything about whether they were going to Columbus or not; it wasn't told [to] them. They only told me they didn't know. I asked them if they knowed they was going into Columbus and they said "no", that they didn't know; Villa had informed all the officers around them and then told the officers what he was going to do and taken each command and came in[.][22]

When asked by the State if the defendants had all admitted that they were in Columbus during the fighting, Fillmore replied that they had.[23]

During cross-examination, Attorney Wood attempted to establish that 1) the defendants knew nothing of Villa's plans, and 2) that the defendants were forced to obey the commands of their officers under pain of death. Fillmore agreed with the Wood's assertions.[24]

The State rested its case, and the Court asked Defense Attorney Wood if he wished to make an opening statement before presenting his case. Wood replied in the affirmative and began the case for the Defense:

> Gentlemen, the defense in this case expects to prove first that these defendants were present in Columbus on the morning of the 9th; that all these boys, these defendants are residents of Old Mexico; that they were illeterate [*sic*] and that xx [the word "if" is crossed out]

18

every one of them as far as miltaryism [sic] is concerned is right now, if he will be permitted to go back into Mexico, a conscripted man. We will expect to prove that all of these defendants were forced and conscripted by Villa or some man under the personal direction of Villa and they were put under arms, and we expect to prove that they were told any attempt upon their part to escape or desert, it simply meant death on their part ... . We expect to prove that the movements of Villa were matters of a mystery to these defendants; that these defendants did not know anything about the country ... they were in. We expect to prove that when the attack was made upon Columbus these defendants were simply acting by virtue of their military orders and that they did not participate in the raid because their military duties did not require that duty of them. We expect to prove that these mexicans [*sic*] came from far down in the interior and as I have stated are illiterate[25] and consequently their military service was[a] compulsory matter kept up and indulged in by them on account of personal threats they would receive from their commanding officer—that in case of desertion they would be shot ... ."[26]

Attorney Wood then called his first witness, Juan Rodriguez.[27]

Under questioning by Attorney Wood, Rodriguez stated that he was taken prisoner by Villa at Santa Ana on February 16, 1916. He was placed under the supervision of a Major and told nothing of Villa's plans. He did not know where he was when following Villa's movements, and he did not fight at Columbus because he was detailed to hold horses. He had a rifle, but no ammunition, and he was in the company of perhaps ten or fifteen other men who were holding the horses of those who were fighting.[28] Those who fought did so on foot, and while he was aware of the fighting he did not know with whom they were fighting. He left in the first retreat, and it was during the retreat that he was wounded.[29]

Under cross-examination, Rodriguez denied he had entered Columbus. He asserted that he had no idea of how far he was from the town, but he could hear shooting and see burning buildings. His rifle, for which he had no ammunition, was on his horse. He denied again knowing with whom Villa's men were fighting and claimed to have no knowledge of looting. He did not, he alleged, know where the international border was, and repeated his claim that he was wounded while riding away from the fighting with those who had fled.

Vaught: "You knew that when you were following Villa, didn't you, that you were going out to fight?"

Rodriguez: "I didn't know that I was coming to fight."[30]

The witness maintained that he did not know Villa was coming to fight Americans, and that he came with Villa as a prisoner and not as a soldier. Rodriguez concluded his testimony by declaring that he and others like him were unable to escape because they were closely watched.[31]

The second witness for the defense was Eusevia Renteria.[32] Under direct examination, he stated that he was in General Francisco Beltran's command and had been with Villa's forces for about three months. He had served five years in the army of Diaz, was discharged and shortly afterwards was taken captive by Yaqui Indians. He remained with them for fourteen months and was taken captive by Villa at a mining camp at Cobrado, having been there less than a month. Villa turned him over to Beltran at San Geronimo, and from there he came to Columbus. Renteria asserted he came with Villa unwillingly; had he resisted he would have been shot. He had no knowledge of where he was or where he was going: "We were always ignorant as to what he [Villa] intended to do. We just marched along when he told us to."[33]

Under cross-examination, the defendant again denied any knowledge of where he was going or what he was going there for.

Vaught: "But you did know, didn't you, that you were out on a mission to make trouble?"

The Defense objected and was overruled by the Court.

Renteria: "Why, no, I wasn't out on any mission; I wasn't—I was there because they made me come."

Renteria admitted he had a Mauser rifle and fifty rounds of ammunition (later reduced to thirty as he had shot or lost some).[34] He denied willingness to use the rifle and ammunition to shoot anyone, but admitted "… with this man [Villa] if you disobeyed him in any way at all he would kill you."[35] He asserted that he was heading in the direction of the fighting when he was wounded. He had not fired a shot, and his comrades carried him away from the fighting.[36]

José Rangel was the next witness for the Defense.[37] Rangel testified that he was working on a ranch, and when he went into Chihuahua City to get supplies Villa captured him. He was pressed into Villa's forces two and one-half months before the Columbus raid. He had not fought for Villa, he asserted, and he did not know where he was going. He was not armed during the first three weeks of his captivity; he had no knowledge of a pending attack upon an American city.

During cross-examination, Rangel testified that he was armed and had ammunition but did not enter Columbus. He was under the command of Juan Martines[z?] and acted as an orderly. His only job was to hold the horses of those who entered the town on foot.[38]

Juan Castillo was the next witness for the defense.[39] Castillo testified that he was serving under General Hernandez of Carranza's forces when he was taken prisoner by Villa at Santa Ana. He was placed under the supervision of Captain Luz Pena, and escape was not possible because he was too closely watched. He told the Court that the Villistas camped during the day and marched only at night, therefore he had no way of knowing where he was or where he was going. Castillo concluded his direct examination by declaring that if he had known the attack was directed at Columbus, an American town, he would not have taken part in the attack.

During Vaught's cross-examination, Castillo declared that he was with the horses. He had been ordered by his captain to remain behind with the horses because he had no ammunition. While holding the horses, Castillo testified, he was wounded and joined in the retreat. He told the Court that before retreating he had heard shooting and had seen fires in Columbus. Vaught asked Castillo if Villa had been present at Columbus, and he responded that Villa had, indeed, been present.[40]

The fifth witness for the Defense was Taurino Garcia.[41] Garcia testified that he was taken captive by Villa in the latter days of January, 1916 while traveling from Chihuahua to Oaxaca. Villa accused him of being a spy for Carranza, and had him beaten and placed in the ranks of his followers. When Villa's army reached San Geronimo, Garcia was turned over to General Beltran's command. The defendant testified that Villa had told him escape was impossible, if he tried he would be executed, and disobedience to a direct order meant death.

Under Vaught's cross-examination, the defendant testified that he was eventually given a rifle and fifteen rounds of ammunition. He denied entering Columbus during the attack, stating that he was wounded shortly after dismounting. He remembered being carried away and claimed his rifle had not been loaded.[42] Garcia was then asked by the Court: "When they collected up the wounded how many did they get of you, the wounded[?]" He replied that about twenty wounded were gathered, and he estimated the number of raiders to have been about three hundred.[43]

The final witness for the defense was Francisco Alvares.[44] In a brief examination by Attorney Wood, Alvares testified that he was never in Columbus, New Mexico, but had remained by a river with a large number of other Villistas.[45] Under cross-examination, he explained that he had been with Villa for about two months, was armed with a rifle and ammunition, but did not know where he was going or why he was going there. He stated he could see houses, but the houses were a long way in the distance.

Vaught: "I will ask you if it isn't a fact that ... Villa ... stop[ped] near the International Line and there [you] heard Villa tell those soldiers that he was going to attack that town and...the bank would be robbed ... that every soldier could help himself ... that they were to shoot every American man they saw ... and that he would give each one of them an American wife; is that or is that not true?"

Defense: "Objection."

Court: "Overruled."

Alvares: "No, that isn't so. He never said anything to us where we were going."

Vaught: "And he didn't tell you to go up there and kill the American men?"

Alvares: "No."[46]

The final witness of the trial was the boy, Jesus Paiz.[47] He was called as a rebuttal witness on behalf of the State. Paiz testified that he and his father had been with Villa for about three months. His father was one of Villa's bodyguards. Shortly before the attack on Columbus, Paiz stated, Villa addressed the men, saying "Viva Mexico and death to the Americans." The men were promised loot, and it was for that reason, Paiz asserted, that many of them left their ranches in Mexico and followed Villa. Under cross-examination by the defense, Paiz testified that men were left behind to care for the horses of those who advanced on foot to fight in the town. Following Paiz' testimony, both the prosecution and the defense rested and were directed by the Court to deliver their closing arguments. The State presented its argument to the jury, followed by Defense Attorney Wood. Attorney Vaught addressed the jury again following the conclusion of arguments for the defense. The arguments of the attorneys have not, unfortunately, survived.[48]

---

[1] The trial transcript is held at the State Records Center and Archives (SRCAA), Santa Fe, New Mexico. A photocopy is in the present writer's possession. Hereinafter referred to as Renteria.

[2] Ralph E. Twitchell, *Leading Facts of New Mexico History* (Cedar Rapid, Iowa: Torch Press, 1917), 376. The conclusions regarding the prosecution's decision are, of course, speculation on the part of the present writer, who has been unable to find documentary evidence offering conclusive proof of the State's strategy.

[3] U.S. Senate, #7665, 1627.

[4] *Ibid.*

[5] *Ibid.*

[6] Renteria, *op. cit.,* 9-11.

[7] See Appendix A.

[8] Trial Commentary, note #1.

[9] Trial Commentary, note #2.

[10] *Ibid.,* 26.

[11] See Appendix B.

[12] Renteria, *op. cit.,* 31.

[13] Hulsey saw Miller's body after the raid was over: "Three balls entered him: one in here—the left shoulder, apparently through the arm and one through the left breast and one through the right breast." *Ibid.,*

[14] *Ibid.,* 40-1. See Trial Commentary #3.

[15] *Ibid.,* 52.

[16] *Ibid.,* 57.

[17] *Ibid.,* 66.

[18] *Ibid.,* 74.

[19] *Ibid.,* 82.

[20] *Ibid.,* 88.

[21] *Ibid., passim,* 92-4.

[22] *Ibid.,* 102.

[23] *Ibid.*

[24] *Ibid.,* 104.

[25] The question of literacy is a source of controversy. The defendants' attorney and those who sought leniency for the Villistas made much of their alleged illiteracy. According to the New Mexico State Penitentiary "Description of Convict" forms, Alvares, Rangel, and Sanchez were illiterate. Castillo, Garcia, Renteria, and Rodriguez were listed as literate and possessed a common school education. The "Description of Convict" forms were filled out for each inmate received and contained basic information. *Penitentiary Record Book of Convicts,* November 2, 1884–September 27, 1917, SRCAA, Santa Fe, New Mexico. Hereinafter *PRBC.* See Appendix C.

[26] Renteria, *op. cit.,* 105-06.

[27] Juan Rodriguez was 20 years old and was born in Nuevo Leon, Mexico.

[28] The fence at the international border had been cut about 2:30 A.M. on March 9 and a force of twenty men remained there as a rear guard. When the attackers reached the dirt road leading to Columbus, another fifteen men were posted. Joseph R. Monticone, "Revolutionary Mexico and the U.S. Southwest: The Columbus Raid" (unpublished MA thesis, California State University, Fullerton, 1981), 74.

[29] Renteria, *op. cit.,* 106-08.

[30] *Ibid.,* 115.

[31] *Ibid.,* 109-16.

[32] Eusevia Renteria was 24 and was born in Morelio, Michoacan, Mexico.

[33] *Ibid.,* 120.

[34] Trial Commentary, note #4.

[35] *Ibid.,* 124.

[36] *Ibid., passim,* 117-31.

[37] Jose Rangel, age 23, was born at Hacienda Chinambas, Jalisco, Mexico.

[38] Renteria, *op. cit.,* 132-37.

[39] Juan Castillo, age 26, was born in Queretaro, Mexico.

[40] Renteria, *op. cit., passim,* 137-44.

[41] Taurino Garcia, age 21, was born in Oaxaca, Mexico. The trial transcript has his birth place as "Yuajaco", Mexico.

[42] Renteria, *op. cit.,* 145-50.

[43] *Ibid.,* 151.

[44] Francisco Alvares, age 22, was born at San Juan del Rio, Durango, Mexico.

[45] Renteria, *op. cit.,* 152-53.

[46] *Ibid.,* 159-61.

[47] See above, page 5, n. 23. In his interesting testimony given before Senator Fall's Senate Subcommittee in 1920, Piaz, then sixteen years old, told of his life following the Columbus raid. After recovering from the

operation severing his left leg, he went to school in Albuquerque for about two years. He worked in a hospital in Gallup, New Mexico, then moved to Deming to attend school. At the time of his testimony before Fall's committee, he was working as a presser in a tailor's shop in Columbus. U.S., Congress, Senate, Subcommittee of the Committee on Foreign Relations, *Investigation of Mexican Affairs*. [66th Congress, 2nd Session, Senate Documents, Vol. IX, 1919-1929, #7665]. Washington: Government Printing Office, 1921.), 1621-22. Hereinafter, U. S. Senate, #7665.

[48] Trial Commentary, note #5.

Chapter 3
Judge Medler Gives the Trial to the Jury

Judge Medler then delivered his detailed instructions to the jury.[1] The indictment, he explained, was made up of two counts: 1) the defendants shot and killed Charles D. Miller, and 2) that the killing was done by some person or persons unknown to the grand jurors, and the defendants "... were present aiding, abetting, [and] were concerned and engaged in the unlawful, deliberate and premeditated killing of the said Miller."[2] He next read the statutory definition of first-degree murder and followed this with definitions of the key words and terms in the indictment.[3] The jury was informed of the differences between the two counts of the indictment, and in the crucial tenth instruction were told "... that in law those who have actually and with their own hands committed the fact are ... principals in the first degree, and those who are present, aiding and abetting at the commission of the fact are principals in the second degree."[4]

In order for the jury to find the defendants liable as principals in the second degree, they must have been *present and aiding and abetting at the fact* of the murder. Judge Medler went on to explain:

> If several persons should set out together, or in small parties, upon one common design, to commit an unlawful act, such as murder, arson, robbery or other felony, or for any other purpose unlawful in itself, and each takes the part assigned to him; some to commit the fact, others to watch at proper distances and stations to prevent a surprise, or to favor, if need be, the escape of those who are more immediately engaged, they are all, provided the fact be committed, in the eye of the law present at it.[5]

He further instructed the jury that a person involved in committing a crime must be a free agent not acting under, or subject to, actual force at the time of the crime. If, however, the force enacted upon a person is a *moral force* "... threatening with duress

27

or imprisonment, or even by an assault to the peril of life, in order to compel a person to commit a crime ... ." constitutes neither a legal excuse for nor a justification of the crime.[6]

In the course of the trial, the defendants had claimed that they were soldiers obeying orders. Judge Medler instructed the jurors that "... in this case you can take into consideration that no state of war existed on the 9th day of March, 1916 ...," and since a state of war did not exist, "... there was no justification in law for a military expedition ..." and certainly no justification for the events that took place in Columbus on that day.[7] Some of the defendants offered as an alibi the claim that they were not present at the scene of the murder. The jurors were instructed that "... if, in view of the evidence, the jury have any reasonable doubt ..." as to the location of the defendants "... they should give the defendants the benefit of any doubt, and find them not guilty."[8] The judge then gave the jurors an explanation of what the law means by *reasonable doubt*:

> A reasonable doubt is a doubt based on reason, and which is reasonable in view of all the evidence. And if, after an impartial comparison and consideration of all the evidence, you can candidly say that you are not satisfied of the defendants' guilt, you have a reasonable doubt; but if, after such impartial comparison and consideration of all the evidence, you can truthfully say that you have an abiding conviction of the defendants' guilt, such as you would be willing to act upon in the more weighty and important matters relating to your own affairs, you then have no reasonable doubt.[9]

In closing his instructions to the jury, Judge Medler instructed them that they had no right to allow either prejudices or sympathies to affect their verdict; neither could they allow the consequences of their decision to affect their verdict. He told them that the penalty under law for conviction in a case of first-degree murder was death, but cautioned them that their verdict dealt only with the guilt or innocence of the defendants. The imposition of the penalty was the responsibility of the Court. The jury was given three forms of verdict: 1) guilty of murder in the first degree as charged in the first count of the indictment, 2) guilty of murder in the first degree as charged in the second count of the indictment, and 3) not guilty. They were free, the judge instructed them, to find one or more of the defendants guilty and one or more of the defendants not guilty. The jury was then given the indictment, the forms of verdict, and the instructions. They were directed upon retiring to select a foreman, who would be responsible for signing the verdict form agreed upon.

The bailiffs were sworn by the Court, and the jury retired at 11:29 A.M. to select a foreman, consider the evidence, and render its verdict. At 11:59, the jury returned to the courtroom; the clerk called the jury roll and all jurors answered present. The Court read the verdict presented by Foreman Albert Field: the defendants were found guilty of murder in the first degree as charged in the second count of the indictment.[10] The jury was discharged, and the judgment and sentence against the defendants "... was duly pronounced by the Court and entered of record in the words following, to-wit:—"

> WHEREUPON, IT IS ORDERED BY THE COURT, and is the Judgement and Sentence of the Court, that the said defendants, and each of them, that is to say, you the said EUSEVIO RENTERIA, TAURINO GARCIA, JOSÉ RODRIGUEZ, FRANCISCO ALVAREZ, JOSÉ RANGEL, and JUAN CASTILLO be remanded to the custody of the Sheriff of Luna County, New Mexico, and that you and each of you, be by him safely kept until Friday the 19th day of May, A. D. 1916, that on said day, between the hours of six o'clock in the morning and six 'clock in the afternoon of said day, in an enclosure to be erected by said Sheriff in the Town of Deming, the county seat of said Luna County, and State of New Mexico, you EUSEVIO RENTERIA, TAURINO GARCIA, JOSÉ RODRIGUEZ, FRANCISO ALVAREZ, JOSÉ RANGEL, AND JUAN CASTILLO be then and there by the said Sheriff of the said County of Luna, hanged by the neck until you are dead, and may God have mercy on your soul.[11]

The trial was over, the prisoners were remanded to the sheriff and the protests began.

[1] Renteria, *op. cit.*, 162-76. There are twenty-six instructions covering fifteen pages in the transcript.

[2] *Ibid.*, 163.

[3] *Ibid.*, 165-66. The words defined were *deliberate, premeditated, unlawfully, feloniously, knowingly,* and *willfully*. He carefully explained the concept of *malice* from the perspective of the law.

[4] *Ibid.*, 168.

[5] *Ibid.* Trial Commentary, note #6.

[6] *Ibid.*, 170.

[7] *Ibid.*

[8] *Ibid.*, 172.

[9] *Ibid.*, 172-73.

[10] *Ibid.*, 184.

[11] Criminal Case #664, Judge Medler to Sheriff Simpson, LCCO.

Chapter 4
Protests Against the Sentences

Following the trial protests against the scheduled May 19, 1916 executions were made. On April 28, 1916, Edward C. Wade, Jr., Santa Fe attorney, sent a telegram to President Woodrow Wilson asking for Wilson's involvement in the fate of the convicted Villistas: "They are ignorant, illiterate, and like children mentally; one is seriously wounded. They were … taken prisoners in Mexico without extradition proceedings and turned over to the state authorities for punishment. They contend they are military prisoners … and should be so treated."[1] Wade asked Wilson to "… urge Governor of New Mexico to grant respite to these men where thorough investigations can be had by federal authorities on law and facts."[2]

Governor McDonald of New Mexico responded to the White House by telegram on May 4, 1916, informing the President that nothing official had come to his office regarding the seven men convicted of complicity in the Columbus murders. McDonald informed the President that the men had been taken by train to the State Penitentiary for safe keeping, their cases would be given careful consideration, and that following an investigation of trials further communications would follow.[3] On May 8, 1916, President Wilson informed Governor McDonald that he was aware of the impending executions of the Villista raiders and asked the Governor to consider deferring the executions until "… the capture of the principal offender, Villa, whose case should be disposed of along similar lines … ."[4] President Wilson expressed concern that the executions might possibly trigger acts of reprisal against American citizens in Mexico and asked McDonald to consider reprieving the Villistas "… for a reasonable period in order that their present execution may not complicate the existing conditions…"[5]

On May 12, 1916, McDonald informed the President that a reprieve would be necessary in order to investigate the cases more thoroughly. His communication to the President continued:

You will readily understand that there is considerable feeling in New Mexico, and I believe these cases should be handled carefully in order to prevent, so far as possible, any objectionable developments here as well as in Mexico. I think, however, I shall be able to handle the cases in such a way as to prevent any serious complications here or in Mexico, and at the same time act in accordance with your suggestion.[6]

The following day, Governor McDonald issued a twenty-one day reprieve for the seven condemned Villistas.

The Villistas' defense attorney, Buel R. Wood, acting on behalf of the Carranza Government of the Republic of Mexico, petitioned Governor McDonald for a stay of execution until such time as Wood could "… present such facts and circumstances as do not constitute any part of the record as made in these cases and make such statements and arguments as will be meet and proper which all shall tend toward the exercise or the attainment of executive clemency …"[7] In the petition Wood did not enumerate which, if any, of the facts or circumstances not in the trial record might lead the Governor to grant the Villistas clemency.

On June 3, 1916, Governor McDonald sent President Wilson the following telegram:

Investigation in cases of Mexicans convicted of murder at Columbus March 9, 1916, shows that they had a fair trial. Perhaps it was a mistake to try cases in [a] border county, but everything appears to have been fair. Six of the men were probably taken in Mexico, but were legally in [the] jurisdiction of court that tried them. Defense was that Villa impressed them into his service and that they did not know where they were. One of them was shown to have been in United States prior to March 9; one admitted to having been close to Miller when he was killed.[8]

The executions were set for June 9, 1916. On Wednesday, June 7, Governor McDonald gave a twenty-one day reprieve to Eusevio Renteria, Taurino Garcia, José Rodriguez, José Rangel, and Juan Castillo. New Mexico National Guardsmen (Company B of Carlsbad and Company I of Deming) patrolled the area near the

32

jail, where the scaffold had been erected.[9] All saloons were closed, and Deming gave the appearance of a town under martial law.[10]

The Santa Fe *New Mexican* of June 9, 1916, carried a page three headline: "Bandits Alvarez and Sanchez Pay Extreme Penalty On Deming Scaffold For Murder Of Columbus Citizens:Villistas Hanged Early This Morning in Luna Jail Yard." Alvarez was the first to be hanged, the *New Mexican* noted, and Sanchez followed shortly. The El Paso *Morning Times* reported that Alvarez stepped to the gallows at 6:34 A.M., the trap was sprung at 6:36 A.M., and at 6:45 he was pronounced dead; Sanchez took his place at 7:10 A.M., the trap opened at 7:13, and at 7:30 A.M. his body was taken down and placed next to his comrade in the jail yard.[11] The El Paso *Morning Times Edicion en Espanol* of July 10, 1916 gave first page, first column, coverage to the executions: "*Los Crimenes Registrados En Columbus Fueron Pagados Por Dos Mexicanos Con Sus Vidas.*"[12] The Spanish edition article went on to say that both men were Villistas who were wounded and captured during the attack on Columbus and were executed in Deming, New Mexico.[13]

After reviewing the trial transcript and speaking personally to Renteria, Garcia, Rangel, and Castillo at the Penitentiary in Santa Fe, Governor McDonald concluded that the evidence connecting the four directly to the raid was persuasive beyond reasonable doubt and ordered their sentences to be executed. On June 28, 1916, McDonald commuted the sentence of José Rodriguez to life in the State Penitentiary. The four condemned men were moved from Santa Fe to Deming for execution.

On the morning of June 30, 1916, Company D of the New Mexico National Guard was in the Deming armory in anticipation of demonstrations. No disturbances occurred, and within the enclosed area at the jail the executions proceeded as planned. The men were hanged in pairs; at 6:00 A.M., the first to mount the scaffold were Renteria and Garcia. They were not pronounced dead until twenty minutes after the trap was sprung.[14] Rangel and Castillo followed their comrades at 7:17 A.M.; the drop broke their necks and death was virtually instantaneous.[15] The only one of the Villistas to escape the gallows, José Rodriguez, was put to work in the Penitentiary brick-making plant. He was, it was reported, in good health and gave promise of being a good worker.

Edward C. Wade, Jr. expressed satisfaction with the commutation of Rodriguez' death sentence, viewing it as a vindication of the movement he initiated to secure a reprieve and a further investigation of the Villistas' case. Wade claimed the evidence presented in the case did not warrant the death penalty for Rodriguez, and while he realized that his course of action in seeking judicial review for the Villistas was extremely unpopular, he "… felt it my duty, as an officer of the courts of New Mexico, to volunteer my services in bringing about a re-examination of the cases."[16]

---

[1] Arthur S. Link, Editor, *The Papers of Woodrow Wilson* (Princeton, NJ: Princeton University Press, 1981), Vol. 36, 566. Hereinafter, *PWW*.

[2] *Ibid.,* 567.

[3] *Ibid.,* May 4, 1916, William Calhoun McDonald to Joseph Patrick Tumulty, 606.

[4] *Ibid.,* 653.

[5] *Ibid.,* 654.

[6] *PWW,* Vol. 37, 31.

[7] Petition to William C. McDonald, Governor of the State of New Mexico from Buel R. Wood, Attorney, Santa Fe, New Mexico, May 15, 1916, 2. SRCAA.

[8] *PWW,* Vol. 37, 159. [1] A footnote appears in the *PWW* explaining that two Millers were killed in the attack: Charles DeWitt Miller and C.C. Miller.

[9] Santa Fe *New Mexican*, June 9, 1916, 3; Silver City *Independent*, June 13, 1916, 3.

[10] Silver City *Independent*, June 13, 1916, 2.

[11] The following week, the Santa Fe *New Mexican*, June 15, 1916, carried a story from the Silver City *Independent* headlined, "Juan Sanchez Had To Be Hanged Twice At Deming, Report: Villista Raider Found To Be Alive After Being Cut Down; Grisley Botch Made Of Execution". The story reported that Sanchez showed signs of life after being cut down, and the sheriff's assistants carried him back to the gallows, readjusted the noose, and hanged him a second time. Neither the *Deming Graphic* nor the *Deming Headlight* mentioned a botched execution. The *Graphic* reported "Everything passed quietly: Sheriff Simpson had everything in perfect readiness and there not one slip in the cog." June 9, 1916, 1.

[12] El Paso *Morning Times Edicion en Espanol*, June 10, 1916, 1.

[13] No relatives came to claim the bodies, and both Alvarez and Sanchez were buried in the potter's field in one of the local cemeteries. Silver City *Independent*, June 13, 1916, 2.

[14] Santa Fe *New Mexican*, June 30, 1916, 3.

[15] *Ibid.* See also the El Paso *Morning Times Edicion en Espanol,* July 1, 1916, *passim*, 1.

[16] *Ibid.*

Chapter 5
The Villista 19[1]

In October 1916, nineteen alleged Villistas captured by the Punitive Expedition were arraigned before the Luna County Grand Jury. The nineteen were indicted for the murders of J.J. Moore (Cause #718), P. Simon (Cause #719), James T. Dean (Cause #720), and C.D. Miller (Cause #721).[2] Mariano Jimenez was indicted for the murder of James T. Dean (Cause #722), and the remaining eighteen were each indicted for the murder of Charles D. Miller (Causes #723-740). In each individual indictment, a person whose name was unknown was also indicted. The Court, Judge Raymond R. Ryan presiding, appointed James S. Casey to defend the alleged Villistas.[3]

The defense entered a Plea to the Jurisdiction of the Court on behalf of each defendant. The defense argued that the Court had 1) no jurisdiction to try and determine the case, and 2) had no jurisdiction over the person, life, or liberty of the defendants, for the two reasons:

1) The alleged offense does not constitute an invasion of the peace and sovereignty of the State of New Mexico.
2) The alleged offense does not constitute a violation of any right secured by the constitution or laws of the State of New Mexico.[4]

The plea to jurisdiction was followed by a Stipulation in which both parties agreed to certain facts in respect to the offense with which the defendants were charged: that the defendants took part in the Columbus raid of March 9, 1916; that in the course of the raid Paul Simon, the deceased named in the indictment, met his death; that prior to the attack the United States had recognized a *de facto* government in the Republic of Mexico; that there had been at a time prior to the raid an American military occupation of the city

These Villistas who raided Columbus, New Mexico, were apprehended in the mountains of Mexico and held in camp near Namiquipa, Mexico. The prisoners are guarded by Buffalo Soldiers of the 24th Infantry Regiment.
Courtesy: National Archive and Records Administration, Still Picture Branch, College Park, Maryland.

Villistas cooking in the stockade at Namiquipa, Mexico.
Courtesy: National Archive and Records Administration, Still Picture Branch, College Park Maryland.

of Vera Cruz, Mexico; that at a time prior to the raid a number of American citizens had been killed at Santa Ysabel, Chihuahua, Mexico; that prior to the attack and as a result of the events and occurrences noted, feelings of hostility developed between the people of the United States and the people of Mexico; that prior to the attack officers of the American Army had been informed of threats to attack the United States made by Francisco Villa, who did in fact conduct such an attack on March 9, 1916; and, finally, that subsequent to the attack the United States launched a Punitive Expedition into Mexico "… for the purpose of effecting the capture, arrest and conviction of the persons taking part in such attack."[5]

Under an agreement reached by all parties, the defendants agreed to plead guilty to a charge of second degree murder in return for a life sentence to the State Penitentiary.[6] When the defendants faced sentencing, one of them, Guadalupe Chavez, demurred: "… after he came into court he changed his mind and while the others indicted with him pleaded with him to go ahead and enter the same plea along with the rest of them, he was very obstinate and refused to do so."[7] Chavez was granted a change of venue to Grant County by Judge Colin Neblitt, 6th Judicial District Court. Of the remaining eighteen, fifteen would be sent to the Penitentiary at Santa Fe on August 28, 1917.[8] The Penitentiary records make no mention of Francisco Herras, Francisco Mejia, and Juan Mesa.[9]

Following incarceration in the State Penitentiary, efforts began to secure pardons for the convicted Villistas. Governor Lindsey received an application for pardon from Juan Muñoz, and in a letter dated May 4, 1918, Judge Ryan of the Sixth Judicial District Court was "… very much in favor of his being pardoned on condition that he be deported by the immigrant inspector."[10] Judge Ryan went on to say that part of the difficulty with the deportation process was finding proof that the petitioner was, in fact, a Mexican citizen: "… on investigation of the files kept by the court, I found no record was kept as to whether any were citizens of old Mexico."[11] Governor Lindsey had contacted the United States Department of Labor, Immigration Service, for the necessary deportation papers in the event of the prisoner's release and was told that the matter was being considered.[12] The question of release and deportation made its way through the bureaucratic

This photograph of the Villista prisoners in the camp near
Namiquipa, Mexico, was taken April 27, 1916.
Courtesy: National Archives and Records Administration,
Still Picture Branch, College Park, Maryland.

corridors of the Immigration Service from New Mexico through Texas to Washington, DC, and in June Governor Lindsey was informed that

> ... the attitude of the Department at Washington is that in view of the facts presented to it in this case, it can not consistently take any action upon which the alien's release from prison might be predicated; in other words, unless and until Juan B. Muñoz is released by the appropriate state authorities, consideration of the question of his deportation cannot be had.[13]

There the question of pardon and deportation apparently came to an end until it was reconsidered by Governor Larrazolo.

---

[1] Alberto Calzadiaz Barerra, author of *Por Que Villa Ataco Columbus,* claims that twenty-two Villistas were brought back by the Punitive Expedition and were incarcerated in the Grant County jail at Silver City under such barbaric conditions that four died of malnutrition and abuse. See Appendix I.

[2] LCCO. The nineteen men were Pedro Borciago, Ramon Bustillos, Tomás Camareno, Guadalupe Chavez, Lorenzo Gutierrez, Francisco Herras, Mariano Jimenez, Pedro Lopez, José de la Luz Marquez, Francisco Mejia, Juan Mesa, Juan Muñoz, David Rodriguez, Raphael Rodriguez, Francisco Solis, José Tena, Juan Torres, Santos Torres, and Silvino Vargas.

[3] The only records extant in the cases of the nineteen alleged Villistas are the grand jury indictments, various court orders moving the prisoners from Deming to the Penitentiary at Santa Fe for safekeeping and back to Deming for trials (LCCO), the New Mexico Territorial Penitentiary Roster, 1884-1917 (SRCAA), and assorted documents related to Cause #1180 through Cause #1187, Luna County Criminal Cases (LCCO).

[4] Plea to the Jurisdiction. Judge Ryan denied the plea.

[5] *Ibid.,* Stipulation.

[6] The specific sentence was a sentence of no less than seventy nor more than eighty years in the penitentiary.

[7] J. S. Vaught to Governor W. E. Lindsey, January 7, 1918. Governor Lindsey Papers, SROAA. The letter was a response to Governor Lindsey's request for information about Chavez, from whom Lindsey had received a letter asking for attention to the fact that there had been no trial. Vaught pointed out to the governor that a trial was not, at that time, possible because most of the witnesses in the case were with the American

Expeditionary Forces in France. The present writer's investigation of the Grant County Clerk's records found no mention of Guadalupe Chavez, nor did the Sheriff's Office have records of Chavev's incarceration.

[8] Borciago (#4071), Bustillos (#4066), Camareno (#4069), Gutierrez (#4074), Jimenez (#4079), Lopez (#4076), Marquez (#4073), Muñoz (#4079), Rodriguez, D. (#4080), Rodriguez, R. (#4075), Solis [Salis in the Penitentiary record] (#4081), Tena [Lena in the Penitentiary record] (#4072), Torres, J. (#4082), Torres, S. (#4070), and Vargas (#4077). *PRBC.* Raphael Bustamente is listed among these Villistas (#4067) as sentenced to seventy to eighty years for murder, but was not indicted with them. *PRBC.* He appears later in Causes 1180-87. LCCO.

[9] No records of the three men were found in the Luna County Clerk's Office (other than the indictments), the Grant County Clerk's Office, or in the SRCAA at Santa Fe.

[10] Governor Lindsey Papers, Penal File, SRCAA.

[11] *Ibid.*

[12] *Ibid.,* V L. Patch, Immigrant Inspector to W. E. Lindsey, April 29, 1918.

[13] *Ibid.,* G.J. Harris, Acting Supervising Inspector, to Governor Lindsey, June 22, 1918.

Chapter 6
The Pardons

In May 1919, Larrazolo was informed that a petition would be filed by A.B. Renehan "... for some form of relief for the so-called Villistas who are confined in the penitentiary, and in my opinion after several exhaustive conferences with them without just cause."[1] Renehan had taken autobiographical statements from each prisoner, and told the governor that the statements would be forwarded to his office.[2] The letter asserted:

> These men are victims of a press-gang, seized by force, under threats and made a part of Villa's army, utterly ignorant of their destination at the time of the Columbus raid, except a general supposition that they were being led to attack Carranza forces supposed to be at Palomas. One poor little devil, who was never even near Columbus, but was pointed out as a Columbus raider by the relatives of a girl he wanted to marry, but against whom there was family opposition, is paralyzed from the hips down. The family used the method of denouncing him as a raider as an easy way of keeping him from getting the girl.[3]

Larrazolo was asked to read the stories of the prisoners carefully as they were "... interesting dramatic and novelesque human documents ... ." and provided a unique insight into the personal equation of revolutionary turmoil.[4]

Through the remainder of 1919 and into 1920, Governor Larrazolo received letters from family members and friends of the prisoners requesting the use of the governor's powers of pardon to alleviate the situation of the imprisoned men. Letters were received on behalf of Ramon Bustillos, Tomas Camareno, Juan Muñoz, David Rodriguez, and others, pleading with the governor to intervene on behalf of the prisoners.[5] Both those who wanted the release of the prisoners and those who opposed such an action

Villista prisoners and guards at Headquarters camp
near Namiquipa, Mexico.
*Courtesy: National Archive and Records Administration,
Still Picture Branch, College Park, Maryland.*

were answered in Governor Larrazolo's *Executive Order* of November 22, 1920.

Beginning his order with a brief summary of the raid on Columbus and General Pershing's subsequent expedition into Mexico, the governor then began his argument in support of his pardon. The men listed in the order were all common soldiers, privates, in the ranks of Villa's army and were subsequently captured in Mexico by American troops of the Pershing expedition.[6] The attorney for the prisoners, A.B. Renehan, assisted by the Mexican Consul in Santa Fe, Carlos Palacios Roji, based his petition on the assertion that the prisoners were innocent of the charges upon which they had been convicted, because they were not responsible agents in what took place at Columbus. Larrazolo's approach was a more detailed one.

A state of war existed, the governor asserted, between the United States and Mexico as a result of the American seizure of Vera Cruz on April 21, 1914. Even though there was no formal declaration of war, a condition of war existed, and if that condition of war existed in 1916, the Villistas were prisoners of war and therefore not liable for trial in a civil court. If, however, "... the relations between our country and Mexico...had been composed at the time the assault upon Columbus was made by the Mexican troops ... this phase of the case now under consideration is not applicable, and becomes absolutely inconsequential and unimportant in deciding it."[7] The decision between a condition of war or a condition of peace between the United State and Mexico was not essential in the pardon proceedings, the governor asserted, because "... there is another point which to my mind is **absolutely conclusive** [emphasis added] in the determination of the proposition of whether or not these defendants are guilty ... ."[8] That point was the rank of the prisoners within Villa's army.

Larrazolo had interviewed each of the Villistas and found 1) they were, with several exceptions, illiterate; 2) they came from among the laboring poor; and 3) all were forced into Villa's service against their will, and by force.[9] Even if they were volunteers in Villa's army, as common soldiers they were bound under military discipline to "... absolute, unconditional and passive obedience ... to ... superior officers ... ."[10] Common soldiers, the governor

Villista Prisoners in makeshift stockade, Namiquipa, Mexico, 1916.
Courtesy: National Archives and Records Administration,
Still Pictures Branch, College Park, Maryland.

Villista prisoners rebuild a building for use as a stockade,
Namiquipa, Mexico, 1916.
*Courtesy: National Archives and Records Administration,
Still Pictures Branch, College Park, Maryland.*

argued, were not informed of "... the maneuvers and movement of troops, that information is never communicated to the rank and file of the army;... ."[11] Villa's army was structured in command as all armies were, the governor continued, and maintained and enforced military discipline that compelled the rank and file to obedience.

The common soldiers were so uninformed, Larrazolo asserted, "It is a fact that when they, in pursuance of superior orders, attacked the town of Columbus, not one of them knew that he was standing on foreign soil and attacking an American settlement ... ."[12] Even if they had known they were attacking an American town, the governor continued, "... still they would not be guilty of murder, because, as stated above, they were not responsible agents ..." because their orders bound them to obedience under penalty of death.[13] Furthermore, in order for a crime to be committed there must have been *malice*, which the governor defined as a willful, deliberate and perverted intention and desire to do wrong on the part of the attackers. We cannot say what was in the hearts and minds of the men engaged in the assault on Columbus, Larrazolo argued, we can only know that they were simply carrying out the orders and commands of their superior officers.

The governor then continued with a reference to the case, *Arce et al., vs. The State of Texas*. The case concerned an attack by Mexican troops on United States soldiers on the Texas side of the Rio Grande. Casualties were suffered on both sides. Six Mexican soldiers were taken prisoner, indicted in the death of an American soldier, tried, convicted of first degree murder, and sentenced to death. The Court of Criminal Appeals of the State of Texas stated:

> When a soldier is ordered to fight, it is his duty to do so, and he may forfeit his life on refusal so to do ... . These Mexican soldiers were ordered by their officers, commanded by the officers, headed by the officers to make the fight; the officers led them into the battle, and they fought. If the state courts had jurisdiction of these defendants, we are of the opinion the conviction is erroneous.
>
> From the viewpoint of this case, we are of the opinion that this judgement should be reversed, and the cause remanded.[14]

With this as precedent, Larrazolo stated his belief that if the prisoners, who had pleaded guilty to murder in the second degree in exchange for a sentence less than death, had had a regular trial based on the facts as known, they would have received a directed acquittal and been set free.[15]

Stating that he was "... absolutely convinced in my own mind that these men are not guilty of murder in any degree ...," the governor granted the sixteen prisoners "... a full, complete and unconditional pardon from the crime of murder for which they were ... convicted ... and of the further service of the sentence imposed upon them ... the same to all intents and purposes as if they had never been convicted as above stated."[16] The Superintendent of the State Penitentiary was directed to act in conformity to the Executive Order once it was signed and sealed by the Secretary of State.

The heart of Larrazolo's argument was that the prisoners were common *soldiers*, not officers, in an organized, structured army with a hierarchy of command from private to general, and that they were simply following orders given them by superiors and therefore could not be held accountable for their actions. They were not *raiders*, *looters*, or *bandits*. The governor did not use the word *raid* to describe the incident, rather he used the word *assault*; the men were *defendants*, not prisoners who had pleaded guilty to second degree murder in exchange for a sentence of life in prison.[17]

The governor must have been unaware of the intense lobbying campaign to secure the release of Juan Muñoz. The effort began in early April 1918, and continued through the remainder of Governor Lindsey's term and into Larrazolo's tenure. An answer to a letter from Muñoz' father, José Muñoz, is worth noting:

> General Headquarters
> American Expeditionary Forces
> Second Section, G.S., G-2
> May 12, 1918
>
> I acknowledge your letter of April 18th, in which you ask me to write the Governor of New Mexico with a view to securing pardon for your son, Juan B. Muñoz, late Lieutenant, Mexican Revolutionary Forces.
> I regret to say that my official position prevents me from

New Mexico State Penitentiary photograph of Lieutenant Juan Muñoz.
Received: 8/28/1917

Age: 25
Height: 5'8½"
Weight: 151
Hair: Black
Complexion: Fair
Read: Yes
Write: Yes
Attended College

Photographs taken at New Mexico State Penitentiary 8/28/1917.
#4067 - Raphael Bustamente: Age: 22, Height: 5'3¼", Weight: 130, Hair: Black, Complexion: Fair, Read: Yes, Write: Yes.
#4071 - Pedro Borciago: Age 24, Height: 5'8", Weight: 138½, Hair: Black, Complexion: Fair, Read: Yes, Write: Yes.

Photographs taken at New Mexico State Penitentiary, 8/28/1917.
#4077 - Silvino Vargas: Age 18, Height: 5'2", Weight: 95, Hair: Black, Complexion: Fair, Read: No, Write: No.
#4080 - David Rodriguez: Age: 23, Height: 5'4¼", Weight: 129, Hair: Black, Complexion: Fair, Read: Yes, Write: Yes.

New Mexico State Penitentiary photograph of Lieutenant Francisco Salis/Solis.

Received: 8/28/1917
Age: 29
Height: 5'5"
Weight: 111
Hair: Black
Complexion: Fair
Read: Yes
Write: Yes
Common School

writing a letter of this nature to the Governor. I can say, however, that Lieut. Juan B. Muñoz, when a prisoner in Mexico, was of great service to the Expeditionary Forces and materially assisted us in the capture of several of the Columbus raiders. You can use this letter in any manner you see fit.

s/N W. Campanole
Major, General Staff, A.E.F.[18]

Here is one Villista, present at Columbus and in prison for his part in the raid, who was not a private.[19]

Another prisoner who was not a private soldier was General Lorenzo Gutierrez. Gutierrez was captured in April, 1916 in a village on the Santa Maria River, about thirty miles northwest of Namiquipa, by Second Lieutenant Norman J. Boots, 10th Cavalry. On the retreat south following the Columbus raid, Gutierrez had carried off a man's wife and child. The husband managed to find them and informed General Pershing where Gutierrez was located. Lt. Boots and his platoon were sent to capture the general and bring him to Pershing. Following a lively skirmish in which the Villista general was wounded, the capture was effected. With Gutierrez, Lt. Boots reported, "... we also found two or three pairs of shoes and a couple of bolts of silk that he had taken from one of the stores in Columbus, N. M. I presumed this was the evidence which later convicted him."[20] The Corporal was also in possession of a Winchester carbine, a gun boot, two cartridge belts, an empty canvas moneybag, and fifty-five rounds of ammunition.[21]

As to Larrazolo's assertion that the attackers did not know they were on American soil, the evidence is mixed. The testimony of Jesus Piaz asserted that prior to the attack, Villa addressed the raiders. Piaz went on to testify that the men had been promised loot, and that was the reason many of them had left their ranches in Mexico and followed Villa. In testimony given years later before Senator Fall's Senate Subcommittee, Piaz reversed himself and said, "... so when we got to Columbus, none of us did not know. There were so many men innocent they did not know they were going to fight Americans. They thought they were going to fight Carranza soldiers on Mexican ground."[22] When asked by Senator Fall if he knew he was in the United States when he got to Columbus, Piaz replied that he did not know he was in the United State until he heard Americans speaking English, which he did not understand.[23] Why his testimony before Fall's committee was so different from that given in the Renteria trial is not clear.

On March 7, 1916, Villa had sent three men into Columbus to observe and report on the military and its activities. They reported to Villa that the town had but a small garrison, a report confirmed by two other men sent by Villa the following day.[24] S.H. McCullough, in his testimony before Fall's committee, stated: "I noticed a good many strange Mexicans in town all day on the 8th and going to work that morning I met two bunches, one four and one three, going to Columbus on foot, and the bunch of three stopped me...they wanted water ... ."[25] The two days immediately before the raid were busy ones for Villa's scouts, it appears, and we can only speculate about the rank of the scouts: were they officers, private soldiers, or both? One thing appears to be certain: relatively large numbers of people immediately south of the border knew of the impending attack.

In testimony before the Senate Subcommittee on Foreign Relations on February 2, 1920, Nils Olaf Bagge, a consulting mining engineer with sixteen years' experience in Mexico, recalled a conversation with an Army captain about Villa's Columbus raid. Bagge had apparently been informed that there were Villistas in Columbus *before* the raid. He could not understand how so many Mexicans could get into town without being noticed and was told it was simple: "... if a Mexican soldier would leave his arms on the other side of the fence ... they could come in ... so there were no doubt a great many Villa bandits within the town ... before the attack ... ."[26] Villa had sympathizers in Columbus, and information about the area was not difficult to obtain.[27]

---

[1] Governor Larrazolo Papers, Penal Papers, November, 1920, A.B. Renehan to Governor Larrazolo, May 13, 1919. SRCAA.

[2] There is no record of the autobiographical statements in the Larrazolo Papers, nor did a search of the available files locate them.

[3] *Ibid.* This story has an apocryphal ring to it. While being interviewed in 1984, Joe Barrales of Tucson, Arizona, told of his grandfather

who was sold to the Colorados by his parents because of a problem with a girl. The girl's parents were after him, "...so they, you know, shipped him off to the army." *Interview With Joe Barrales, Tucson, Arizona, 14 June 1984*, History File #26, SRCAA, 2.

[4] *Ibid.*

[5] *Ibid.*, November 22, 1920, Capture and Pardon of Men in Villa Raid, SRCAA. Not all communications present in the Capture and Pardon File reflect sentiments for the release of the Villistas. The Commander of the New Mexico Department of the American Legion and the Commander of the Claude Close Howard Post #2 of Deming, New Mexico sent the governor angry letters of protest.

[6] The exception was José Rodriguez, who was found guilty of murder in the first degree in an earlier trial (State of New Mexico vs. Eusevio Renteria, *et als.* Luna County Criminal Case #664), sentenced to hang, and whose sentence was commuted by Governor McDonald.

[7] *Ibid.*, 4.

[8] *Ibid.*, 5.

[9] A description given by Friedrich Katz of the social composition of Villa's armed forces between the dissolution of the División del Norte and the withdrawal of Pershing's expedition (a time which included the Columbus attack) is worth mentioning here. "It [Villa's armed force] now consisted of a heterogeneous mix of veterans of the División del Norte (largely Dorados) whose loyalty to Villa transcended every other loyalty, of villagers taking up arms after having been despoiled of their belongings by Carrancista soldiers, of federal deserters who preferred the gold paid by Villa to Carranza's worthless paper money, and by an increasing number of out-of-work cowboys." Friedrich Katz, *The Life and Times of Pancho Villa* (Stanford University Press, 1998), 802. Hereinafter *Pancho Villa*.

[10] *Executive Order, op.cit.,* 5.

[11] *Ibid., 6.*

[12] *Ibid., 7.*

[13] *Ibid.*

[14] *Ibid., 9.*

[15] *Ibid.* He believed this because Judge Raymond R. Ryan, who had passed sentence on the prisoners, told the governor that in his opinion the men should be pardoned. Ryan could not speak for José Rodriguez, however, as Rodriguez had been part of a different trial with a different judge.

[16] *Ibid., 10.*

[17] The prisoners could not have been ignorant of the fate of the men who earlier had been tried before a jury, found guilty, and sentenced to death. The six hangings were certainly no cause for optimism on the part of the nineteen who faced trial in the same courtroom. There must have been compelling motivation to accept the bargain offered.

[18] Governor Lindsey Papers, *op. cit.,* N. W. Campanole to José Muñoz, May 12, 1918.

[19] In addition to Lt. Muñoz, Borciago, Bustamente, Vargas, D. Rodriguez, and Solis were reported as Lieutenants. *Deming Headlight,* History File #26, SRCAA.

[20] Tompkins, *op,cit., 205-06.* "In any case," the lieutenant continued, "I turned him over to General Pershing and was informed later he had been sentenced to life imprisonment at Deming, N.M."

[21] National Archives, Record Group 395, Box 1, E-1210: Headquarters Historical Data, Punitive Expedition to Mexico Headquarters, 1916-17, "Record of Prisoners". Corporal Gutierrez claimed that all the goods found in his possession were given to him by José Gutierrez upon return from Columbus. *Ibid.*

[22] U. S. Senate #7665, 1617-18.

[23] *Ibid.,* 1618. The testimony of other witnesses before Fall's committee gives the impression that the raiders knew where they were and had a definite plan of attack. See the testimonies of S.H. McCullough, Lee Riggs, Laura Ritchie, and Archibald B. Frost, *passim,* 1584-1616. The absence from school of the Mexican children from Palomas who attended school in Columbus on the day before the raid was noted in the testimony of L.L Burkhead, 1606. Their absence suggests, perhaps, that their parents knew that something potentially dangerous was about to happen.

[24] James A. Sandos, "German Involvement in Northern Mexico, 1915-1916: A New Look at the Columbus Raid," *Hispanic American Historical Review* L:1 (February 1970), 77. Sandos' sources are Alberto Calzadiaz Berrera, *Villa contra todo y contra todos: en pos de la venganza sobre Columbus, N.M.* (Mexico, 1960) and Pershing Papers, Box 372.

[25] U.S. Senate, *op. cit.,* 1586. McCullough was a section foreman for the El Paso and Southwestern Railroad.

[26] U.S. Senate #7665, 1434-35. From the context of the conversation, the captain was either Rudolph E. Smyser or George Williams (Tompkins, *op. cit.,* 55.)

[27] Mitchell Yockelson, "The United States Armed Forces and the Mexican Punitive Expedition," *Prologue* 29:2 (Fall 1997), 259.

Chapter 7
Reaction to the Pardons

Governor Larrazolo's pardon was greeted with mixed reactions throughout the state. The Santa Fe *New Mexican* reprinted the governor's pardon along with six photos of three of the hanged Villistas with the headline, "FACES OF VILLISTAS BEAR OUT CLAIM OF IGNORANCE."[1] The article following the headline and the three penitentiary identification photos of the Villistas called the men "… specimens typical of sixteen convicts who received pardons from Governor Larrazolo."[2] Less sympathetic to the governor was New Mexico's American Legion.

The New Mexico American Legion Department Commander, J. W. Chapman wrote Larrazolo, "… I cannot imagine any facts which could be presented to you which would … induce you to exercise executive clemency to men who have been convicted of the murder of innocent AMERICAN MEN, women, and children."[3] Commander Chapman wrote on behalf of Legion members throughout the United States, many of whom "… were called to protect American citizens on the Mexican border from the attacks of murderers such as these. I protest against the issuance of pardons to these men."[4] The Carl McDermott Post #26 of Portales, New Mexico, forwarded resolutions denouncing the pardons and calling for the Lt. Governor to convene an extraordinary session of the Legislature to begin impeachment proceedings against Larrazolo.[5] The Claude Close Howard Post #2 of Deming condemned the pardons as "… a traversity [*sic*] on justice and an open insult to the American soldiers through the conceding to ruthless brigands a status of beliggerency [*sic*] which they could not have possessed either in the Republic of Mexico nor in the United States of America."[6]

The release of the prisoners had been scheduled for Thanksgiving Day, 1920, but was delayed until December 4, as a result of an injunction issued by Judge Reed Holloman of the district court.[7]

The injunction was issued on the application of Edward I. Safford, who acted on behalf of the Hugh Carlisle American Legion Post of Albuquerque. In the opinion of attorneys questioned, the Villistas could be charged with the murder of any other of the victims of the raid by the next meeting of the grand jury, "… providing Luna county is willing to undertake the expense of the prosecution. It was pointed out, however, that the original prosecution put a considerable dent in that county's court fund."[8]

On November 24, Acting Governor Benjamin F. Pankey was asked by Attorney Neil B. Field to halt the release of the Villista prisoners (Governor Larrazolo was in Mexico). Fields, at the head of a delegation from Albuquerque, repeated his request of Pankey on November 28, asking the acting governor to revoke Larrazolo's pardons. Pankey, after consulting with a representative of the Attorney General's Office, concluded he had no power to interfere, and Assistant Attorney General Harry S. Bowman asked for time to make an investigation of Field's brief.

On December 4, 1920, the day the district court's temporary injunction expired, and during Governor Larrazolo's absence in Mexico, Acting Governor Pankey ordered the Acting Superintendent of the State Penitentiary "… to hold said prisoners until the further orders from the Executive of this State, or from the Courts."[9] The day before his Executive Order was delivered to the penitentiary Pankey had been informed by Attorney General O.O. Askren that the office of Acting Governor had no authority to revoke the pardons. The controversy became moot, however, when Judge Reed Holloman made the temporary injunction permanent until such time as the matter could be taken up by the New Mexico Supreme Court.

Shortly after his return from Mexico, Governor Larrazolo issued an *Executive Order* to the Superintendent of the State Penitentiary to "… disregard the aforesaid executive order of the Acting Governor Benj. F. Pankey, dated as aforesaid, on the 4th day of December, A. D. 1920, and unless prevented by superior force or authority, to give full force and effect to, and obey the order given by me…November 22, 1920 …" and release the sixteen prisoners in custody.[10] Before the order was executed, the sixteen prisoners were re-arrested by a Luna County Deputy Sheriff, thus giving the

Supreme Court another problem to ponder: if the governor is within the limits of his power in pardoning the prisoners, is the Sheriff of Luna County within the limits of his authority in arresting them?

The re-arrest of the Villistas followed murder indictments for fifteen of the men and a warrant issued on a complaint filed by District Attorney A.S. Vaught for the other. The warrants made the same charge against all sixteen: murder as the result of the death one of the fifteen Americans killed in the raid on Columbus by Francisco Villa. Although Luna County had at first balked at the prospect of the expense of another trial, the re-arrests were seen as an indication that the county was willing to bear the expense rather than see the Villistas released through the governor's pardon.

---

[1] Santa Fe *New Mexican*, November 22, 1920, 1.

[2] *Ibid.* Whether this statement was influenced by nineteenth-century *phrenology* (the study of the conformation of the skull based on the belief that it is indicative of mental faculties and character) or by racial prejudice, the present writer will leave to the reader's judgment.

[3] Larrazolo Papers, *op, cit.,* Chapman to Larrazolo, November 24, 1920.

[4] *Ibid.*

[5] *Ibid.,* T. J. Molinari to Larrazolo, November 26, 1920. The resolution asserted that Larrazolo pardoned the Villistas because he planned to return permanently to Mexico, "...the home of his birth, and having in mind the hope that his insult to this country will tend to his personal aggrandizement in Mexico."

[6] Larrazolo Papers, *op. cit.,* Walter Clark, Adjutant, to Larrazolo, December 7, 1920.

[7] Santa Fe *New Mexican,* November 26, 1920, 1. The injunction was issued Wednesday, November 24, 1920, and was in effect until December 4, 1920, on which day the court would decide to make it permanent or dissolve it.

[8] *Ibid.,* November 27, 1920, 1.

[9] Larrazolo Papers, *op. cit.,* Benjamin F. Pankey to P. J. Duggin, December 4, 1920. Governor Larrazolo had departed the United States via train from El Paso, Texas, on November 26, 1920, to attend the inauguration of President-elect General Obregon (Santa Fe *New Mexican,* November 26, 1920, 1).

[10] Larrazolo Papers, *op. cit.,* Executive Order to Fidel Ortiz, Superintendent, State Penitentiary, December 16, 1920.

Chapter 8
The Supreme Court's Decision

The most important question before the Supreme Court was the meaning of Section 6, Article 52 of the State Constitution: "Subject to such regulations as may be prescribed by law the governor shall have the power to grant reprieves and pardons, after conviction for all offenses except treason and in cases of impeachment." What, precisely, did the constitutional convention mean by the wording of the article, specifically the first section: "Subject to such regulations as may be prescribed by law . . . ."? Does it suggest that the legislature has the right to limit the power of the governor, subjecting his pardoning power to legislative limitations, or does it refer only to conditions included in the pardons themselves?[1] Put another way, is the power to pardon as described in the constitution invested exclusively in the governor? The hearing was set for December 16, 1920, in the Supreme Court.[2]

On December 28, 1920, the Santa Fe *New Mexican* reported, "PARDONING POWER OF GOVERNOR IS ABSOLUTE: Cannot Be Restricted by Legislative Act; Were Bandits, Declared; Mexicans Will Remain in State Prison for Safe-Keeping."[3] While the governor's power to pardon was valid,[4] the power to arrest the Villistas before they could be released was also valid, the Court declared. In the decision, written by Chief Justice C.J. Parker, the Court called Villa a "notorious bandit", and the pardoned men ". . . members of a marauding band of Mexicans, [who] killed a number of our citizens without conceivable cause or provocation."[5] The Court referred to the raiders as a "company of bandits", who were not entitled to "consideration or protection from criminal prosecutions accorded to members of a recognized military organization."[6] The Court further justified the injunction, which prevented the release of the prisoners, as well as the validity of their arrest by Luna County authorities.[7]

Governor Larrazolo's last official statement before retirement appeared in the Santa Fe *New Mexican*. It was a defense of the pardoned Villistas, a history of Francisco Villa's role in the Mexican Revolution, and an argument in support of his pardons. "The punishment of these men ... for the unjust conduct and actions of Francisco Villa will be a rank injustice and a blot on civilization," the governor asserted.[8] He was convinced that a fair trial for the Villistas was impossible because the Supreme Court had branded Villa a "notorious bandit" and his followers as "marauders." The Court, Larrazolo argued, had no business offering such gratuitous commentary in proceedings which "... were purely, solely and exclusively questions of law, touching the power of the governor to grant pardons ... ."[9] In doing so the Court had so prejudiced the issue in the eyes of the public that no fair trial of the prisoners was possible, and it was, therefore, necessary for the governor to present his case to prove that they were not bandits.

When Francisco Villa visited El Paso, Texas, some years before the affair at Columbus, he had been enthusiastically hailed by his hosts as the "Napoleon of Mexico", and by October, 1914, he was the Chief of Military Operations of the Convention Party. In 1915, Villa commanded an army of perhaps 40,000 men, and the consular representatives of Great Britain, France, Germany, and the United States recognized him as the general of an army. He had led his army in a number of operations against the Constitutionalist forces of General Obregon: Mexico City, Ramos Arispe, Celaya (twice), Agua Prieta, Alamito, and Fort Sin. With Obregon's defeat of General Rodriguez at Cima, December 9, 1915, Villa's power in Sonora came to an end.

Why, asked Larrazolo, in the light of his record as commander of an army, should Villa be considered a "bandit" for his attack on Columbus? Columbus "... was a military expedition, pure and simple, and nothing else, for which Villa [w]as and is responsible, but certainly not the common soldiers ... he was the commander of a regularly organized army, and ... the men under him were regular army soldiers."[10] The Supreme Court argued that had the Villistas been members of the army of a recognized government of the Republic of Mexico, the episode would have grounds for war.[11] "That is exactly what resulted from the attack on Columbus,"

Larrazolo argued, "because even though Villa's army was not the army of any government recognized by us, yet it resulted in the Pershing expedition into Mexico, which was nothing else but an act of war against that country." [12]

---

[1] *Ibid.,* "Villista Case Puts Important Question Up To Supreme Court", December 10, 1920, 3.

[2] Appearing for the Mexican government were A. B. Renehan, and former Attorney General N. D. Meyer. Attorney General O. O. Askren and Assistant Attorney Harry S. Bowman appeared for the Acting Warden of the Penitentiary, P. J. Duggan, who was the other party to the action. *Ibid.,* December 16, 1920, 1.

[3] *Ibid.,* December 28, 1920, 1.

[4] Chief Justice C. J. Parker wrote: "...the ultimate power and right to pardon is granted, unrestrained by any consideration other than the conscience and wisdom and sense of public duty of the Governor. No other board or person is to be consulted, nor is their approval to be obtained. The decision rests solely with the executive." *Ex parte* Bustillos, 26 N.M. 450, *New Mexico Reports: Reported Cases Determined in the Supreme Court of the State of New Mexico, 1920-1921*, Vol. 26, 449-69; Albuquerque, NM: Central Printing Company, 1921, 459.

[5] *Ibid.,* 455.

[6] *Ibid.*

[7] "From all of the foregoing it appears that the petitioners, notwithstanding the pardons issued by the Governor are not now entitled to be discharged from custody by reason of their subsequent arrest and commitment to the custody of the superintendent of the penitentiary, and that the writ of habeas corpus should be discharged and the petitioners remanded to custody; and it is so ordered." *Ibid.,* 469.

[8] Santa Fe *New Mexican,* December 31, 1920, 1.

[9] *Ibid.*

[10] *Ibid.* The governor offered no explanation of Villa's objectives in the attack on Columbus. A "military operation, pure and simple" would, it seems, have had *military* objectives (e.g., elements of *tactics* and/or *strategy*) similar to what General Villa had had in earlier operations against Carranza and Obregon. Villa's motives and objectives in the Columbus raid have, of course, been the subject of lively and, at times, heated debate between and among scholars of the Mexican Revolution on both sides of the border: *cf.,* "Communications", *The American Historical Review* 84:1 (February 1979), 304-07 for an exchange between James A. Sandos and Friedrich Katz.

[11] *NMR,* 455.

[12] Santa Fe *New Mexican,* December 31, 1920, 5. From its inception, the mission of the Punitive Expedition suffered from a number of misconceptions. Initially General Funston's orders called for capturing Villa and preventing further raids by his forces. These orders were given to the press as official policy *before* General Scott's orders arrived overruling the original orders. Scott's orders called for the dispersal of Villa's forces, and they did *not* call for capturing Villa. (*cf.* Michael L. Tate, "Pershing's Punitive Expedition: Pursuer of Bandits or Presidential Panacea?", *The Americas* 32:1 (July 1975), 54-5.) In a "Not For Publication" release to the representatives of the press, the White House announced that the proposed expedition was not an invasion and did not pose a threat to the sovereignty of Mexico: "... the expedition is simply a punitive measure aimed solely at the elimination of the bandits who raided Columbus and who infest an unprotected district along the border and use it for a base of operations against American lives and property in the United States." (*cf. PWW*, Vol. 36, 351.) On March 25, 1916, in a release published in the *New York Times,* President Wilson stated, "...the expedition into Mexico was ordered under an agreement with the defacto Government of Mexico for the single purpose of taking the bandit Villa..." (*Ibid.,* 364-65) Small wonder there was so much confusion about the primary objective of the expedition! *Cf.* Appendix E.

Chapter 9
The Final Trial

On February 12, 1921 the Villistas in the State Penitentiary at Santa Fe were returned to Deming, New Mexico and placed in the Luna County jail. The movement of the prisoners and the forthcoming trial brought letters of concern from the Mexican Consuls at both El Paso, Texas and San Antonio, Texas.[1] Judge Ryan assured the Governor that the complaints of the prisoners were greatly exaggerated: "I am personally acquainted with conditions at the Deming jail, and it is one of the best conducted jails in the state. Prisoners are receiving plenty of wholesome food, they all wear a regulation prison garb and have clean and good underwear."[2] The Sheriff of Luna County, P.L. Smyer, assured Judge Ryan that since the Villistas had been in his jail "... they have always received ... the same treatment, the same clothing, and the same kind and quantity of food as the other prisoners, and that they ... have never made any complaint to me ... or to any other person in the jail ... ."[3] Sheriff Smyer's report was forwarded to Governor Mecham by Judge Ryan.[4]

In the April 1921 term of the Sixth Judicial Court of the State of New Mexico for Luna County, the Grand Jury returned indictments of sixteen Villistas in four cases of murder.[5] One of the sixteen indicted was José Rodriguez of the Columbus Seven, whose death sentence had been commuted in 1916 by Governor McDonald to life imprisonment in the Penitentiary. They were indicted for the murders of Walton Walker (twice), James T. Dean, and Bessie James. Raphael Bustamente was named alone in four subsequent indictments for the murders of William T. Ritchie (Case #1184), James T. Dean (Case #1185), Bessie James (Case # 1186), and Walton Walker (Case # 1187).

The Court, Judge R.R. Ryan presiding, proceeded to try the sixteen on Cause #1182, the murder of W. T. Ritchie.[6] Forrest Fielder, District Attorney for Luna County who prosecuted the case, stated he would ask for a verdict of murder in the first degree with either the death penalty or acquittal. R.F. Hamilton was appointed by the Court to represent the defendants. Vicente Visconte, Mexican Consul at Columbus, conferred with Attorney Hamilton, April 25, 1921, on behalf of the defendants and informed Hamilton that no aid for the defendants from the Mexican government could be expected. The District Attorney expressed confidence in a conviction of the Villistas, despite a mood of apathy observers sensed in Deming.[7]

Judge Ryan initially expressed doubts about obtaining a jury in Luna County after fourteen of the first nineteen men examined for duty were disqualified. Most of the disqualifications were because of preconceived ideas of the guilt or innocence of the Villistas, the rest for their opposition to the death penalty.[8] Court was recessed to assemble a special venire, and by 2:20 on the afternoon of April 26 the jury had been selected. Among the witnesses were more than a dozen residents of Columbus, Army officers from Washington, DC and Maria Borciago, sister of one of the defendants.[9] The prosecution was searching for Mrs. Maude Meadors, a witness that District Attorney Fielder hoped would give testimony that the raiders had been told by Villa's officers of their destination.[10]

Major N. W. Campanole, Chief of Intelligence on Pershing's staff during the punitive expedition testified as the trial opened on the morning of April 27, 1921. Campanole testified that fifteen of the sixteen defendants admitted their participation in the Columbus raid, and they were identified from photographs taken of them at the expedition's headquarters in Namiquipa, Chihuahua, Mexico. In cross examination, Defense attorney Hamilton brought out that most of the Villistas on trial were conscripted into service by Villa's officers. Major Campanole asserted, however, that fifteen of the men on trial had served under Villa prior to the conscription for the raid on Columbus. The trial went to the jury late in the afternoon of April 28, 1921.[11]

The trial judge, R.R. Ryan, indicated that four verdicts were possible: first or second-degree murder, manslaughter, or acquittal. The defense objected to the submission of second-degree murder and manslaughter, the objection was sustained by the Court, and the case was submitted to the jury as first degree murder with a verdict of either death or acquittal. After twenty-five minutes' deliberation, the jury Foreman, Hugh L. Ramsay, returned the verdict of "Not Guilty".[12]

The Mexican Consul at Columbus stated that the trial had been conducted in the fairest manner possible, and that the result "... will do more than anything that has happened in the past ten years to establish better understanding between the United States and Mexico."[13] Defense attorney Hamilton applauded the jurors for seeing that the evidence did not show the defendants' active participation in the raid, and for understanding that whatever part they had in the affair was forced upon them by Villa. Attorney A.B. Renehan of Santa Fe, who had represented the Villistas earlier but had not taken part in the trial, praised the people of Luna County for "... feeling that it would be unfair to make victims of these 'privates' in Villa's army who acted under fear of their lives, while their leaders were honored and rewarded."[14] He also asserted that the verdict was a clear indication that the American people were essentially just, and that Governor Larrazolo's pardons had been vindicated. On April 30, 1921 the free men, accompanied by the Mexican Consul at Columbus, Vicente Visconte, Jr., crossed the international bridge into Mexico.

Perhaps the most compelling element of the trials and punishments of the Villistas is the question of justice. American citizens and soldiers died in an unprovoked attack on a town of little, if any, military significance. The attack came before dawn, while virtually the entire unsuspecting population was asleep, and the attackers paid a grim price for the assault: sixty-seven Villistas were killed and seven captured.[15] General Pershing's "Punitive Expedition Report" puts the figure at ninety killed (which includes those who died of their wounds) and twenty-three wounded.[16] Seven American troopers were killed and five wounded. One wounded trooper subsequently died at the Fort Bliss Military Hospital. Nine civilians were murdered in the course of the raid, property was destroyed, and looting occurred.[17] The subsequent trials of the accused Villistas raised a number of legal and moral questions as old as the history of civilized conflict.

[1] M.C. Mecham, Penal Papers, "re Villistas and José Rodriguez", correspondence between Governor Mecham and Judge Raymond R. Ryan, March 28 and April 7, 1921, SRCAA.

[2] *Ibid.*, Ryan to Mecham, April 7, 1921, SRCAA.

[3] *Ibid.*, Smyer to Ryan, April 9, 1921, SRCAA.

[4] *Ibid.*, Ryan to Mecham, April 15, 1921, SCRAA.

[5] Luna County Criminal Cases #1180, #1181, #1182, and #1183. Those indicted were Pedro Borciago, Raphael Bustamente, Ramon Busitillos, Tomás Camareno, Lorenzo Gutierrez, Mariano Jimenez, Pedro Lopez, José de la Luz Marquez, Juan Muñoz, David Rodriguez, José Rodriguez, Raphael Rodriguez, Francisco Solis, José Tena, Juan Torres, and Santos Torres. LCCO.

[6] Raphael Bustamente, *et als.* Luna County Criminal Case #1182, LCCO.

[7] *The New Mexican,* April 24, 1921, 1. "Time has assuaged the feeling of the people...[R. F. Hamilton] Most of us would like to forget the Columbus raid. The average citizen registers indifference. It would be a good solution, many say, to take the Villistas 35 miles south to the Mexican border and 'head them south'.", 1.

[8] Santa Fe *New Mexican*, April 26, 1916, 3. Fifty-two prospective jurors were examined before the panel was selected.

[9] *Ibid.*

[10] *Ibid.* Mr. and Mrs. Meadors had been captured in Mexico by Villa. Mr. Meadors was murdered, and Mrs. Meadors escaped at Columbus during the raid.

[11] Santa Fe *New Mexican*, April 27, 1920, 1. Since no trial transcript has survived, we are limited to surviving newspaper accounts for information about testimony. Unfortunately, precious little testimony is available to the contemporary researcher.

[12] Luna County Criminal Case #1182, LCCO. The trial had cost Luna County $3,757.75.

[13] Santa Fe *New Mexican*, April 30, 1921, 1.

[14] *Ibid.*

[15] E. Bruce White, "The Muddied Waters of Columbus, New Mexico." *The Americas* 31:2 (July 1975), 78 (*cf.* Sandos, *supra,* 2, for a higher count of Villistas killed). Several of the prisoners were wounded. The names and penitentiary numbers of the Columbus Seven are found in Appendix F; the names and penitentiary numbers of the Villistas returned from Mexico by the Pershing expedition are found in Appendix G.

[16] Pershing, "PER", 97.

[17] U. S. Senate, #7665, 1623. They were N.T. Ritchie, H.H. Walker, Charles DeWitt Miller, Dr. H.M. Hart, James T. Dean, J.J. Moore, Mrs. M. James, C.C. Miller, and Harry Davis.

Chapter 10
The Hague Conventions,
International and Military Law

In response to the atrocities committed in the Boer War and the conduct of American troops in the Philippines in the course of the Spanish-American War, impetus was given to international activity in the field of developing and applying the laws of war. The immediate result was the Hague Conventions of 1899 and 1907. The Hague Conference Conventions of 1907 contained Convention IV: "Convention Concerning the Laws and Customs of War on Land," to which, along with forty-four other nations, the United States and Mexico were signatories (both nations signed Convention IV without reservation).[1]

The Convention, in Article I, spoke of laws, rights and duties of war that applied not only to armies, but also to militia and volunteer organizations fulfilling the following conditions:

1) To be commanded by a person responsible for his subordinates;
2) To have a fixed distinctive emblem recognizable at a distance;
3) To carry arms openly; and
4) To conduct their operations in accordance with the laws and customs of war.[2]

Article 28 declared: "The pillage of a town or place, even when taken by assault, is prohibited,"[3] as was confiscation of private property.[4] One problem in applying this to the Villista raiders of Columbus rests, at least in part, with establishing their identity: were they soldiers as defined in Article I: 1-4, above, or were they bandits looking for loot? If they were the latter, there are, apparently, no provisions for them in international law; if they were the former, they were subject to personal conduct under a complex code over which even experts find no agreement. Assuming that the Villistas were *soldiers* who met the criteria of Convention IV, Article I, and who thereby came under the 1907 Hague Conventions, how may we assess their subsequent treatment by American authorities? Were they or were they not, *as individuals*, responsible for the murder, arson, and looting that characterized the attack on Columbus, New Mexico? To answer these questions, we must look at the complex domain of international law as it pertains to war.

The case for the defense presented on behalf of the Villistas was, as we have seen, based on the doctrine of *obedience to superior orders*: the defendants in doing the prohibited acts were merely acting in obedience to orders from a military superior.[5] This is one of the most complex technical problems in international law as it relates to warfare, and it first drew attention in the United States in 1804 in the case of *Little v. Barreme.*

An act of Congress had forbidden American ships from trading with France and, through the President, issued orders to armed American ships to examine American vessels "…suspected of such prohibited commerce, and permitted their capture and forfeiture if they were found sailing *to* a French port."[6] A ship sailing to the United States was seized, taken to Boston, and impounded. The ship turned out to be Danish, she was restored, and the owners sued the officers of the American ship for damages. The officers' defense argued that they were following orders issued by the President through the Secretary of the Navy. Chief Justice Marshall, speaking in 1804 for the Supreme Court, concluded "… the instructions cannot change the nature of the transaction, or legalize an act, which, without those instructions, would have been a plain trespass."[7] It made no difference that the officers thought they were acting under the law, because the order they obeyed was subsequently declared by the Court to be unlawful and "… they were held personally liable in damages for acts done in obeying it."[8] *Little v. Barreme* became a landmark case in civil suit adjudication.

Another early decision bearing on the superior orders doctrine was *Ensign Maxwell*, decided in a Scottish court. During the Napoleonic wars, French prisoners in a jail in Scotland failed to extinguish a light in their cell window when ordered to do so. Ensign Maxwell ordered a guard to shoot at the light and a prisoner was killed. Maxwell was tried and convicted for murder before the High

Court of Justiciary, which rejected his plea that he was following orders from a higher authority. The Court's charge to the jury was:

> If an officer were to command a soldier to go out to the street, and to kill you or me, he would not be bound to obey. It must be a legal order given with reference to the circumstances in which he is placed; and thus every officer has a discretion to disobey orders against the known laws of the land.[9]

Both the Scottish Court and the United States Supreme Court were in agreement that there exists no justification for obeying an unlawful order.

In the American case *United States v. Jones*, a case of "privateering" during the War of 1812, the obedience to superior orders doctrine was denied. The case involved crew members of an American "privateer" who stopped a neutral vessel on the high seas, abused the captain and crew, and stole some valuables. At their trial, the crew contended that they had obeyed their captain's orders, and Circuit Justice Washington in charging the jury, said:

> This doctrine, equally alarming and unfounded,... is repugnant to reason, and to the positive law of the land. No military or civil officer can command an inferior to violate the laws of his country; nor will such command excuse, much less justify the act. Can it be for a moment pretended, that the general of an army, or the commander of a ship of war, can order one of his men to commit murder or felony? Certainly not ... . We do not mean to go further than to say, that the participation of the inferior officer, in an act that he *knows, or ought to know to be illegal*, will not be excused by the order of his superior.[10]

This also seems to undercut the defense of *ignorance or mistake of facts*. If the average soldier would have known then and there that the act was illegal, then the accused individual "... is seemingly *chargeable at his peril with knowledge of the unlawfulness of the ordered act.*"[11] Had the legality of the order, however, been open to reasonable doubt, acquittal should follow, because the soldier could not then be expected to have known that it was in fact illegal.

In 1851, in *Mitchell v. Harmony*, a case growing out of the Mexican War regarding theft of private property by an American Army officer in Mexico, the Supreme Court denied the doctrine of obedience to superior orders. Chief Justice Taney wrote:

> Upon principle, independent of the weight of judicial decision, it can never be maintained that a military officer can justify himself for doing an *unlawful* act by producing the order of his superior. The order may palliate, but it cannot justify.[12]

This civil decision is a stricter rule than that in the Jones case, a criminal procedure.[13] In a number of lower Federal court decisions, the obedience to superior orders doctrine was also rejected, and the most authoritative decisions have held defendants to strict criminal liability if an obeyed order turned out to have been, in fact, illegal.[14] What, however, has been the situation in military law?

Neither the original Lieber Code of the American Civil War,[15] nor the revised Lieber Code of 1898 made mention of the doctrine of superior orders.[16] It may be presumed that military commissions and courts-martial followed the precedents established in American judicial decisions. By the turn of the century, however, the doctrine of *honest belief* had made its way into English law. In a case stemming from the Boer War, *(Regina v. Smith)* a soldier who, under orders from a superior killed a native in a trivial dispute, was tried for murder. He was acquitted, and the court stated:

> I think it is a safe rule to lay down that if a soldier honestly believes he is doing his duty in obeying commands of his superior, and if the orders are *not so manifestly illegal* that he must or *ought to have known* that they were unlawful, the private soldier would be protected by the orders of his superior officer.[17]

In 1914, the British *Manual of Military Law* for the first time included a rule on superior orders, as did the *Rules of Land Warfare* of the United States Army.[18]

In post-World War I Germany, however, the situation was different. Two German submarine officers were put on trial for machine-gunning helpless survivors of a torpedoed Canadian

70

hospital ship, the *Llandovery Castle*. They claimed the defense of superior orders, which was rejected by the German Supreme Court:

> Military subordinates are under no obligation to question the order of their superior officers, and they can count upon its legality. But no such confidence can be held to exist if such an order is *universally known to everybody, including also   the accused, to be without any doubt whatsoever against the law* .... They should, therefore, have refused to obey. As they did not do so, they must be punished.[19]

Here we see an example of international law being applied to an individual.

In a later case, the torpedoing of the hospital-ship *Dover Castle*, the Court took a different view of applicability of the German Military Penal Law. The German Admiralty had issued memoranda which charged that the British were using hospital ships for military purposes, thus making such ships legitimate targets for reprisals. The Court acquitted the defendant because he "… did *not know* that in ordering the torpedoing of British hospital ships it was the Admiralty's intention to commit a crime."[20] The Court asserted the defendant's

> conduct clearly shows that this was his conviction … .
> The accused accordingly sank the "Dover C a s t l e" in obedience to a service order of his highest superior; an order which he considered binding. He cannot, therefore, be punished for his conduct.[21]

While civil courts have been fairly consistent on the question of superior orders, military courts have been ambiguous.

---

[1] James B. Scott, *The Hague Conferences of 1899 and 1907* (Baltimore: The Johns Hopkins Press, 1909), II, Table of Signatures, no page number.

[2] Leon Friedman, *The Law of War: A Documentary History* (New York: Random House, Inc. 1972), I, 313-14.

[3] *Ibid.,* 319. Article 47 states simply: "Pillage is formally forbidden." 322.

[4] *Ibid.,* Article 46, 322.

[5] This argument was, as we have also seen, the basis for A. B. Renehan's petition for pardons and Governor Larrazolo's subsequent pardon of the imprisoned Villistas. *Cf.* 34-37.

[6] Shelden Glueck, *War Criminals: Their Prosecution and Punishment* (New York: Alfred A. Knopf, 1944), 144.

[7] *Ibid.,* 145.

[8] *Ibid.*

[9] *Ibid.,* 145-46.

[10] *Ibid.,* 146.

[11] *Ibid.,* 147.

[12] 13 Howard (1851), 115, 137.

[13] Glueck, *op.cit., passim,* 146-49.

[14] *Ibid.,* 148-49; *cf.* fns. 21, 22, 23, 24, and 25; 237-39.

[15] Friedman, *op.cit.,* "The Lieber Code, Washington D. C., April 24, 1863," 158-86. This code is the one on which subsequent codifications of the rules of warfare are based. *Cf.* Glueck, 142.

[16] Glueck, *op.cit.,* 142.

[17] *Ibid.,* 150.

[18] Adopted in 1914, paragraph 347 of the United States Army's *Rules of Land Warfare* stated: "...Individuals of the armed forces will not be punished for these offenses in case they are committed *under the orders or sanction of their government or commanders." Ibid.,* 140. There is an obvious tension between the *Rules* and the earlier judicial decisions.

[19] Judgment in the cases of Lieutenants Dithmar and Boldt, 16 *American Journal of International Law* (1922), 674, 708, 721-22. The Court added: *The rule of international law, which is here involved, is simple and is universally known. No possible doubt can exist with regard to its applicability.* Quoted in Glueck, *op. cit.,* 152, fns. 37, 39; 240.

[20] *Ibid.,* 153.

[21] *Ibid.,* 154, fn. 41; 241.

Chapter 11
Soldiers, Guerrillas or Bandits?

In his pioneering books on banditry, Eric Hobsbawm observed, "The Mexican Revolution contained two major peasant components: the typical bandit-based movement of Pancho Villa in the north, the entirely unbandit-like agrarian agitation of Zapata in Morelos."[1] Villa was recruited by Madero's representatives during the Mexican Revolution, and he accepted the invitation because, in part, it honored his standing in banditry. He became a successful revolutionary general, and "Perhaps of all the professional bandits in the western world, he was the one with the most distinguished revolutionary career."[2] Professors Harris and Sadler write of Madero's recruitment of "guerrilla chieftans," among whom was Francisco Villa.[3] These "irregular commanders" had, by March, 1911, gained control of much of Chihuahua and "... were shattering much of the mystique of Diaz' invincibility."[4] With the fall of Ciudad Juarez and the exile of Diaz, civil war erupted, and the Revolution began to consume its own.

Villa was Commander of the Division of the North, and his reputation and power reached a zenith following his victory at Zacatecas in June 1914. With the fall of Huerta, the civil war continued after a brief pause, with Carranza and Obregon pitted against Villa and Zapata. Villa was driven back to Chihuahua "... reducing him to the status of a regional chieftain, like Zapata."[5] The United States recognized Carranza as *de facto* president of Mexico and permitted him to move troops to Augua Prieta on American railroads. Villa attacked Agua Prieta late in October 1915, and was defeated, thanks in part to the *carrancista* reinforcements.[6]

Following his defeat at Agua Prieta,

> Villa became a forager and a looter—a bandit [and reports] ... from Cananea, Imuris, Magdelena, and Santa Cruz state that "all stores have been looted" and even private dwellings were "cleaned out of everything of

value" and "the whole country denuded of everything edible or of any value."[7]

He managed to extort money, food, and horses from the Cananea Consolidated Copper Company near Naco, and thus replenished, decided to attack Sonora's capital, Hermosillo.[8] The decision cost Villa not only the support of General Jose Rodriguez, who was encamped at Bacoachi, on the upper Sonora River with over half of the Division of the North, but led him to a shattering defeat from which he never recovered.[9] General Obregon "... concluded that Villa had gone insane. The same soldiers who had followed Villa to Sonora with the hope of returning him to national power now declared he had 'entirely lost his mind and [was] almost a raving maniac.'"[10]

According to Enrique Krauze, Villa had become the wild animal he had been just before the Revolution. He felt betrayed and would trust no one:

> He would disappear at night, always sit with his back to the wall, never eat until one of his men had tasted all his food .... The greatly reduced number of followers he has left called him 'The Old Man'. They did not lose their faith in him, but they did lose their identity. If Villa was now an outlaw, what were they? Revolutionaries or bandits?[11]

Following his defeat at Hermosillo, Villa's retreat into Chihuahua was "... at the head of what was now only a large guerrilla band,"[12] and was characterized by atrocities which began at La Colorada with the murder of sixteen Chinese. Some of the hapless victims were shot, some were hanged and a few were pulled apart by horses.[13] The violence reached its nadir in the massacre at San Pedro de la Cueva. The villagers had mistaken several of his men for marauders, and several were killed. In reprisal Villa murdered between seventy-one and eighty-three men by firing squads. The women and girls (and the boys who were to be too young to be considered fighters) were spared. He did not, however, spare the village priest, Father Andres Abelino Flores, whom he personally shot in the head as the priest approached him in an attempt to ransom those not already murdered.[14]

Further banditry "... continued in Chihuahua during 1916, and the looting was so complete that 'not a grain of corn nor article of clothing' was left behind."[15] By January, 1916, "... Villa's mind plunged to new depths of unreality." In a letter to Emiliano Zapata, Villa called for the unification of his own forces with those of Zapata's, "... and together start the work of reconstruction and enhancement of Mexico, punishing our eternal enemy [the United States], the one that has always been encouraging the hatred and provoking difficulties and quarrels among our race."[16]

The source of Villa's anger was his belief in a corrupt bargain between Carranza and the Wilson Administration, a bargain that would have destroyed Mexico's sovereignty. No such bargain existed, nor had one been contemplated, but Villa's imagination, perhaps as Naylor has suggested, was out of touch with reality and had "... ceased to be ruled by fact and began outwardly to act the part of what he was—a haunted, reckless man, desperate to redeem himself by punishing his perceived conqueror, the United States."[17] Naylor anchors Villa's growing frustration firmly in the background of his disastrous Sonora campaign, to "... the fact and extent of his weakened mental state and eroded sense of security."[18] It was Sonora, Naylor argues, that destroyed Villa:

> In Sonora, Villa lost his capacity for responsible leadership. He became instead a callous, vindictive demon ... [he] sank to depths he never reached again ... [he] methodically massacred nearly eighty of his own countrymen; he coldly murdered blameless noncombatants, the exact class of people for whom he ostensibly risked his life in the Revolution.[19]

The failures, the defeats, and the growing pressures of leadership as he tried vainly to keep his dwindling forces together made Villa "... a desperate and depraved man, a man void of reason, haunted by defeat and ruled by revenge."[20]

With his raid on Columbus the following March, Francisco Villa completed a cycle: from pre-Revolutionary bandit to Revolutionary general, to regional chieftain, to guerrilla leader, and back, by late 1915, to bandit. The men who followed Villa to Columbus were both the tiny remnant of a revolutionary army and a collection of freebooters, soldiers of fortune, and impressed peasants held together, we have been told, by either loyalty to, or abject fear of, a man whose ruthlessness was legendary.[21]

In a band as small as Villa's at Columbus, it is difficult to believe that operational plans could for long have been kept from the rank and file (as we have seen, many of the citizens of Palomas knew that something dangerous was about to happen).[22] Mrs. Maude Wright, whose husband had been murdered by the Villistas several days before the attack on Columbus, and who was freed by Villa as the attackers retreated, later said: "From the first I knew that Villa intended to attack Columbus. It was freely discusst [sic] *by the men* and officers [emphasis added]."[23] If we accept Tompkins' assertion that Villa had planted spies in Columbus prior to the raid[24] and had intelligence regarding the layout of the town, then Villa's plan of attack may be regarded as one of *carefully selected targets*, (the evidence bears this out).[25] Under such a carefully developed plan, the attacking forces (***all*** *of the attacking forces, from top to bottom*) would, of necessity, have been instructed accordingly.

There seems to be little if any confusion over Villa's plan. The raiders crossed the international border west of the Palomas gate and

> ... sifted across the border in small bands, united at a point safe from observation from our patrols, then marched northeast until within about one half mile of the American camp when they split into two attacking columns. The first column moved to the south of camp, then east and attacked the stables from a southeasterly direction. The second column crossed the drainage ditch immediately west of the camp at the custom house, where they divided, the first half attacking the camp from the west and the second half moving into town where they proceeded to loot, murder, and burn.[26]

Friedrich Katz, whose revisionist thesis that Villa's primary motivation for the attack on Columbus "... was Villa's firm belief that Woodrow Wilson had concluded an agreement with Carranza that would virtually convert Mexico into a U.S. protectorate,"[27] presents evidence that Villa had informed his troops of his intentions to attack the United States.[28] The original target had been Presidio, Texas, but Villa's plans had to be changed following the desertion of some of his forces. He became increasingly reserved about the next target, and "It was only when they arrived near Columbus, New Mexico, that his men found out where they were going."[29]

In his recently published biography of Villa, Katz states that "Before sending his men across the border, Villa felt that he had to give them some explanation for his decision to attack the United States."[30] His earlier speeches detailing secret agreements between Carranza and Wilson had fallen on either deaf or indifferent ears, and he realized that in order to arouse his soldiers' fighting spirit a new approach had to be taken. He delivered

> ...a rousing speech to his soldiers, calling them to attack the Americans. The only motive he mentioned was revenge. The United States, he said, had been responsible for their defeat at Agua Prieta in Sonora by allowing the Carrancistas to travel across its territory and reinforce the garrison. This accusation elicited a strong reaction from his men, many of whom had participated in the battle of Agua Prieta. Villa also accused the United States of sending defective arms and ammunition to him and thus contributing to his defeat.[31]

If Katz is correct, the Villistas knew *where* they were, where they were *going*, and *why* they were going there. They were neither dupes nor dolts; only when the shadow of the gallows or the prospect of life in prison touched them did they claim to be both.

---

[1] Eric Hobsbawm, *Bandits* (New York: Delacort Press, 1969), 93. Hobsbawm pioneered the concept of the *social bandit*: "...peasant outlaws whom the lord and state regard as criminals, but who remain within peasant society, and are considered by their people as heroes, as champions, avengers, fighters for justice, perhaps even leaders of liberation, and in any case as men to be admired, helped and supported." 13. *Cf.* Hobsbawm, *Primitive Rebels: Studies in Archaic Forms of Social Movement in the 19th and 20th Centuries* (News York: W.W. Norton & Company, 1965).

[2] *Ibid.*, 90.

[3] Harris and Saddler, *op. cit.*, x.

[4] *Ibid.*

[5] *Ibid.*, xiii.

[6] The battlefield was also illuminated with powerful searchlights, which

not only turned the night into day, but also blinded the attackers. Francis J. Munch, "Villa's Columbus Raid: Practical Politics or German Design?", *New Mexico Historical Review* XLIV:3 (July 1969), 193.

[7] *Ibid.,* 192. For a different assessment of Villa, *cf.* Friedrich Katz, "Pancho Villa," in George Wolfskill and Douglas W. Richmond (Eds.), *Essays on the Mexican Revolution: Revisionist Reviews of the Leaders* (Austin & London: University of Texas Press, 1979): Villa :...was not a single-minded bandit and plunderer....[he] was a genuine social reformer who made a large-scale attempt to redistribute the wealth of the rich to the poor....[he was] a social bandit, a peasant leader, a traditional caudillo, a charismatic spokesman for the poor, and an administrator with at least some of the traits of a modern manager." 42-3.

[8] Thomas H. Naylor, "Massacre At San Pedro de la Cueva: The Significance of Pancho Villa's Disastrous Sonora Campaign," *The Western Historical Quarterly* VIII:2 (April 1977), *passim,* 131-33.

[9] *Ibid.,* 134-36.

[10] *Ibid.,* 137.

[11] Enrique Krause, *Mexico: Biography of Power: A History of Modern Mexico, 1810-1996* (New York: Harper Perennial, 1998), 328-29.

[12] Harris and Sadler, *op.cit.,* xiv.

[13] Naylor, *op.cit.,* 130.

[14] *Ibid., passim,* 140-47.

[15] Munch, *op. cit.,* 192. Munch cites the Records of the Department of State Relating to the Internal Affairs of Mexico, 1910-1929; *cf.* 206, fn. 21.

[16] White, *op. cit., 98.* The letter is published in its entirety in White's essay (Villa to Zapata, San Geronimo, January 8, 1916, Adjutant General File 2384662, Record Group 94, National Archives. *Cf.* Harris and Sadler, *op. cit.,* 101-12). How Zapata was to cross the seven to eight hundred miles of Carrancista territory to reach Villa (assuming he was willing) was not discussed.

[17] Naylor, *op. cit.,* 150.

[18] *Ibid.*

[19] *Ibid.*

[20] *Ibid.*

[21] *Cf.* testimony of Eusevia Renteria, 16-17.

[22] *Cf.* 41, fn. 161.

[23] Charles C. Clendenen, *The United States and Pancho Villa: A Study In Unconventional Diplomacy* (Ithaca, New York: Cornel University Press, 1961), 244.

[24] Tompkins, *op.cit.,* 46. Clendenen, *op.cit.,* 240 and Katz *op.cit.,* 563 both discuss spies and intelligence prior to the raid.

[25] Munch, *op.cit.,* 198-200; Clendenen, *op.cit.,* 240.

[26] Tompkins, *op.cit.,* 48-9. See Appendix H.

[27] Katz, "Pancho Villa and the Attack on Columbus," 102. No such an agreement existed, but Katz argues that "... Villa had reasonable

grounds for supposing that it did. In light of this supposition, his actions can no longer be construed as the blind revenge of an unprincipled bandit. They must be viewed as a calculated effort to safeguard what Villa believed others had blindly surrendered— Mexico's independence." For another point of view, see Krauze: "With Pancho Villa almost anything is possible, but to attribute rational realpolitik to his actions is going more than a little too far. Most likely his attack on Columbus was motivated by human passion, for revenge." Krauze, *op. cit.,* 328.

[28] *Ibid.,* 116. Juan Caballero, a participant in the raid, stated that "... Villa concentrated a large part of his troops at the Hacienda de San Jeronimo and told them he planned to attack the United States. Again, the main reason he gave was the secret U.S.-Carranza pact." Katz cites Confederacion de Veteranos Revolucionarios de la División del Notre, Relato de Hechos Historicos de la Actuation del Gral. Francisco Villa y sus Tropas, Archivo de la Palabra Mexico. Typescript by Juan Caballero (December 7, 1941).

[29] *Ibid.,* 117.

[30] Katz, *Pancho Villa,* 563.

[31] *Ibid.,* 564. The paragraph from which this quotation was taken conludes with a curious equivocation: "... there are some indications that ... Villa never told his soldiers that they were crossing the border, and that many continued to believe until the end that they were attacking a Mexican town garrisoned by Carrancista troops."

Chapter 12
Conclusion

The Villista raider who was tried in the first trial and those tried in the second trial were caught either flagrante delicto or in the course of the immediate pursuit by hastily assembled elements of the 13th Cavalry. Their participation in the raid was never in question. Only the nature and extent of their participation was open to interpretation, and that question was what the trials were really about. The decision to try the remaining prisoners together was most certainly a matter of economics: the expense of separate trials and the daily cost of maintaining the accused securely while they awaited trial was simply more than Luna County's treasury could bear.

The Columbus raid was a bloody, violent and destructive affair. Citizens were murdered, and for no discernible reasons; property was looted and destroyed; soldiers lost their lives in defense of the small community. Emotions ran high, not only in Columbus and the Southwest but also in the United States generally. As we have seen, the question of the possibility of a fair trial was on the minds of many observers. We have also seen that Judge Medler carefully instructed the jury in the technicalities of the law. Indeed, it is difficult to imagine a more impartial and detailed set of instructions. The brevity of the jury's deliberations, however, has been seen by some as evidence that the jury's mind was made up before Judge Medler's instructions began. We cannot, unfortunately, get into the minds of the jurors, but it may be just as reasonable to assume that the preponderance of evidence convinced them so conclusively that long deliberation was unnecessary as it is to assume that they had prejudged the accused. The question is of course moot, and each reader will take away from the narrative of the trial his or her own judgment.

The opposition to the execution of the convicted Villistas was a reflection of the hostility to capital punishment that had been growing nationally in the later years of the nineteenth century. Closely connected to that opposition was the reformist consciousness of the opening years of the twentieth century and its association with the new sociological and psychological theories of the perfectibility of both man and society. The biblical admonition of an eye for an eye was being contested by a new "progressive" view: man as victim of overpowering social and mysterious mental forces beyond his control. The old idea of individual responsibility was being challenged by the view that society is the shaping force in human destiny and that people are really pawns in a chess game over which they have no control. The new *criminology* (a word invented in 1890)[1] was billing itself as the scientific study of crime as a *social* phenomenon, and the old idea of punishment was giving way to the new idea of rehabilitation.

Many New Mexicans were concerned about their new state's reputation as a wild and lawless remnant of the Old West. They believed, at least in part correctly, that statehood had been delayed by the nation's perception that New Mexico was simply too lawless and violent, too *uncivilized* to be admitted to the company of the other states. The hangings of the convicted Villistas would, they believed, simply reinforce that perception and cast all New Mexicans into the shadow of national approbation.

Attention began to shift from the victims of the bandits' raid to the perpetrators and soon, in the eyes of some New Mexicans, the perpetrators became the victims (a phenomenon not unfamiliar in our own time). Arguments to spare the convicted murderers were replete with the vocabulary of the new rehabilitative criminology: *ignorant, illiterate, poor, childlike, uneducated,* and *persecuted.* The arguments in behalf of the convicted Villistas were often patronizing and condescending. Governor Larrazolo's arguments in his justification for pardoning the prisoners under life sentences in the penitentiary preceded the defense at the famed Nürnberg Trials (1945-46), and they were no more convincing then than they would prove to be at Nürnberg.

The Columbus 19 were taken by the Punitive Expedition in Mexico, and their capture and arrest was the result of a number of factors. They were turned in by their neighbors who knew they had been on the raid; they were found as a result of the intelligence gathered by the Army; and they were ferreted out by the local militias. All admitted to having been at Columbus during the raid but denied culpability in the violence and mayhem. In return for a life sentence they saved Luna County the expenses of a trial or trials and themselves from a possible trip to the gallows. Since the Luna County jail was too small to hold them securely, they were incarcerated at the Silver City jail pending shipment to the State Penitentiary at Santa Fe.

The local Mexican population of Silver City was permitted to bring them baskets of food to supplement their diet as they had complained of being fed only twice a day. They also complained of having no sugar for their coffee. Standard jail procedure when inmates did not work was two meals a day, and in an economy not far removed from the days of the frontier sugar was considered something of a luxury for prisoners (many if not most citizens did without sugar as part of their daily diet). When the prisoners were taken to Santa Fe they were greeted by the Superintendent and informed that they would be fed twice a day. They were then assured that should they choose to volunteer to work in one of the penitentiary's shops they would be fed three times a day. They all chose to work.

Jails and prisons in the early twentieth century were for the most part Spartan institutions. The new criminology had not yet convinced the authorities in charge of penal institutions that prisoners should live in comfortable surroundings with many of the amenities of the "outside" world. Punishment was the guiding principle, and the idea of rehabilitation had not yet taken hold. The Villista prisoners were treated in the same manner as the other prisoners and if the treatment they received seems harsh from today's perspective, it is because the standards were different. As one jailer rather succinctly put it, prisoners were in the cafeteria to be fed and not to get fat, and the chaplain was available to listen to complaints.

Governor Larrazolo's desire to pardon the Villista prisoners led, as we have seen, to the final trial in Deming in 1921. Five years had done much to dull the once-sharp interest in the affair. No transcript of the trial exists, and the newspaper accounts gave little of the testimony in their daily reporting. We will never know what the jurors thought when Judge Ryan upheld the defense attorney's objection to the submission of second-degree murder and manslaughter to the possible verdicts of first degree murder and acquittal. Defense attorney Hamilton gambled on an all-or-nothing strategy and he won. Faced with the choice between death and freedom for the Villistas, the jurors chose freedom.

The Villistas who were executed had been apprehended either during or immediately after the raid. Those who were tried in 1921 had been brought back from Mexico and perhaps their immediate association with the raid was not seen as clearly as had been the case in the first and second trials. They had also spent several years in prison and that was perhaps seen as punishment enough. The comments attorney Renehan made about the verdict as having vindicated Governor Larrazolo's pardons were self-serving: there is no evidence to indicate that the jurors were influenced by the pardons one way or another. His reference to the prisoners as privates in Villa's "army" indicates either a complete ignorance of the facts or a willingness to distort the truth to the advantage of his position.

When the freed Villistas crossed the international border on April 30, 1921 the Columbus affair came to an end. The law in all cases had been served; the more abstract concept of justice will probably continue to be debated.

---

[1] Webster's *Ninth New Collegiate Dictionary* (Springfield, MA: Merriam-Webster Inc., 1991), 307.

Trial Commentary

Jonathan D. Hurst
Assistant State's Attorney
Morgan County (Jacksonville), Illinois

1). Why Defense Attorney Wood refused to have the State's witnesses placed under the rule is puzzling. Under the rule, any possible prosecution witness to the case is excluded from the courtroom until he testifies, and he cannot discuss his testimony with the other witnesses. This is an advantage for the defense, because the defendant becomes the only witness (should he choose to testify) in the case with an opportunity to hear the testimony of all other witnesses. The resultant advantage is that the defendant is the only witness with an opportunity to "shape" his testimony to more credibly fit the other evidence presented. Also, since the prosecution's witnesses are aware only of their own testimony and of no other, this often makes it possible for the defense to find and point out contradictions potentially damaging to the prosecution's case.

2). Perhaps the defense attorney's worst move, outside of not demanding separate trials and attorneys for each defendant, was his failure properly to question the prospective jurors. The jurors were asked *collectively* several times by the Court if they were prejudiced or biased to the extent that they could not be impartial, and their response was a *collective* silence (Renteria, *op. cit.,* 25-6). They were not *individually* questioned by the defense, nor were there any peremptory challenges used by the defense.

3). Here we see one of the key reasons why separate trials should have been demanded: a co-conspirator's statement cannot be used against an individual defendant unless they are part of the same trial (See Court's: "Were all six of them together[?]", 42.). If separate trials are held, only the defendant's statements may be used against him. If a co-conspirator is called as a witness, he could assert his Fifth Amendment right not to testify and any prior statement he made could not be used unless he made a contradictory

85

statement in the trial, which he would not do if he were asserting his Fifth Amendment right not to testify. For several of these defendants, the statements their co-conspirators made to the State's witnesses would never have been admitted at their (separate) trials, and some of the statements were damning.

4). Renteria's credibility was seriously damaged with this testimony. He first said he had shot some of the fifty rounds of ammunition issued to him (he did not indicate where or at whom he had fired them); he then testified that he "...had lost some of them; some of them got out of my belt[.]" *Ibid.,* 125. Coming from a man with five years' army service, this was probably difficult for the jurors to believe.

5). The arguments were probably not recorded, as they do not constitute evidence.

6). This was an explanation of *accomplice liability,* and in all probability one key to the jury's decision to convict. In the 11th instruction to the jury, *felony murder* was explained. Under New Mexico Statutes (Modern), "New Mexico is one of the few states having a statute which purports to make all murder perpetrated in the commission of or attempt to commit any felony first degree murder." (23) For a complete discussion of felony murder see *New Mexico Statutes 1978 Annotated,* Chapter 2, Homicide, Part A, 14-202., Felony murder; essential elements, (22-23).

Chronology

1916

March 9	Francisco "Pancho" Villa attacked Columbus, New Mexico.
March 15	The Punitive Expedition began.
April 14	Juan Sanchez, Pablo Sanchez, Jesus Paiz were indicted for murder (Pablo Sanchez and Jesus Paiz were not tried).
April 15	Alvarez, Castillo, Garcia, Rangel, Renteria, and Rodriguez were indicted for murder (with Juan Sanchez, they are the "Deming 7").
April 19	The trial of six Villistas began.
April 20	The trial of six Villistas ended with a verdict of "Guilty."
April 24	The six guilty Villistas were sentenced to hang May 19, 1916. Juan Sanchez was found guilty and sentenced to hang May 19, 1916.
May 13	Governor McDonald issued a twenty-one day stay of execution.
June 9	Francisco Alvarez and Juan Sanchez were hanged in Deming, New Mexico.
June 28	The "Columbus 19" were taken to Silver City jail (according to Calzadiaz Berrera). The sentence of José Rodriguez commuted to life in prison.
June 30	Renteria, Garcia, Rangel, and Castillo were hanged in Deming, New Mexico.
October 11	The "Columbus 19" were indicted for murder.

1917

February 5	The last units of the Punitive Expedition returned to Columbus, New Mexico.
February 25	The "Columbus 19" were taken to the State Penitentiary (Calzadiaz Berrera). There is no record of these men in the Penitentiary Roster at that time.

August 27	Eighteen Villistas plea-bargained for life in prison. Guadalupe Chavez was given a change of venue to Silver City.
December 22	Letter from Governor Lindsay regarding Guadalupe Chavez (in Grant County jail) received by District Attorney J.S. Vaught.

1920

November 22	Governor Larrazolo issued a full, complete, and unconditional pardon of Villistas in the State Penitentiary.
December 4	Acting Governor Pankey ordered Penitentiary Asst. Superintendent Dugan to hold Villistas until further orders.
December 16	Governor Larrazolo ordered the Penitentiary Superintendent to disregard Pankey's order and to obey the order of November 22, 1920. Before Governor Larraolos's order could be executed, the Villistas were rearrested by a Luna County Deputy Sheriff and served with indictments for murder.
December 28	The New Mexico Supreme Court declared that both the governor's power to pardon and the county's power to arrest were valid and ordered the Villistas held in the Penitentiary.

1921

February 12	The Villistas in the State Penitentiary were returned to Deming, New Mexico and lodged in the Luna County jail.
April 1	In the April 1921 term of the Sixth Judicial DistrictCourt, the Grand Jury indicted the Villistas for murder.
April 26	The trial procedure of the indicted Villistas began.
April 27	The trial of the Villistas opened.
April 28	The jury returned a verdict of "Not Guilty".
April 30	The sixteen freed Villistas were returned to Mexico.

Appendix A

State of New Mexico vs. Eusevia Renteria, *et als.*
Luna County Criminal Case #664
April 19, 1916[1]

Juror List

Name	Residence in New Mexico	Occupation
Dornbush, Louis	10 years	Farmer
Chase, E.M.	15 years	Farmer, Dairyman
Field, Albert	7 years	Cigar dealer
Haskins, C.W.	34 years	Farmer
Holstein, Sim	19 years	Livery stable operator
Hon. Leroy	9.5 years	Farmer, driller
Maisel, George	5.5 years	Farmer
Phillips, George	4 years	Stock handler
Sandquist, C.R.	5 years	Machinist
Shaw, Wright	5.5 years	Farmer
Wells, William	4 years	Automotive livery
White, A.S.	8 years	Farmer
Parish, F.C.	2.5 years	Merchandising

---

[1]State of New Mexico vs. Eusevia Renteria *et als.* Defendants, Luna County Criminal Case #664, April 16, 1916, 2-25. State Records and Archives, Santa Fe, New Mexico.

[2]Prosecution challenged for cause. Parrish stated he could not sentence a man to death regardless of the evidence. The court sustained the challenge, and Parish was excused. *Ibid., 9-11.* See text, 7.

Appendix B

State of New Mexico vs. Eusuvio Renteria *et als.*
Luna County Criminal Case #664
April 19, 1916[1]

Witnesses for the Prosecution[2]
(In order of Appearance)

Name	Residence	Occupation
Hulsey, T.A.	Columbus, New Mexico	Constable, City
Riggs, L.A.	Columbus, New Mexico	Deputy Collector of Customs
Aguirre, B.S.	Columbus, New Mexico	Custom[s] Service Line Rider
Lemmon, P.K.	Columbus, New Mexico	Merchandising
Fillmore, Lurid	Columbus, New Mexico	Army Corpsman[3]
Pias [Piaz], Jesus[4]	Chihuahua, Mexico[5]	

---

[1]State of New Mexico vs. Eusuvio Renteria, *et als.* Defendants, Luna County Criminal Case #664, April 19, 1916, 2-25. State Records Center and Archives, Santa Fe, New Mexico.

[2]*Ibid.,* 26-105.

[3]Fillmore told the Court he had been in Columbus for ten days. He had been in the Army for twenty-three years as a corpsman and had been sent from El Paso, Texas to the hospital at Columbus to assist in caring for the wounded. *Ibid.,* 95.

[4]Jesus Pias [Piaz]was called by the Prosecution as a rebuttal witness. He was a twelve year old boy who was with his father. *Ibid.,* 159-60. The boy's father, Captain Piaz, was an aide to Francisco Villa. Captain Piaz was killed in the raid, and the boy was wounded when he entered Columbus looking for his father. As a result of his wound, Jesus lost a leg. See Tom Mahoney, "The Columbus Raid," *Southwest Review*, 17:2 (January 1932), 169.

[5]In testimony given before the U. S. Senate Subcommittee on Foreign Relations, Sen. A. B. Fall, Chairman, on February 7, 1920, Jesus stated he was born in Tampico, reared in Durango, and with his father joined Villa's forces in Quintas Carolinas, Chihuahua. Jesus testified that he and his

father joined Villa because it was the only way they could be safe from the Carranzistas who had already killed his three brothers. 66th Congress, 2nd Session, 1919-1920, Senate Documents, Volume 9, *Investigation of Mexican Affairs*, Volume 1, #7665, 1616-17.

Appendix C

New Mexico State Penitentiary.

DESCRIPTION OF CONVICT.

No. _____ Name _____

County received from _____ Date of receipt _____

Sentence _____ Date of Sentence _____

Crime _____ Plea at trial _____

Sex _____ Age _____ Build _____

Nationality _____ Where born _____

In New Mexico _____ years.   In United States _____ years.

Previous convictions _____

In other prisons _____

Trade or occupation _____ Religious instruction _____

Habits _____ Read _____   Write _____ Education _____

Smoke _____ Chew _____   Liquor _____ Drugs _____

Married or single _____   Children _____

Parents _____   Conjugal _____

Father born in _____   Mother born in _____

Relatives _____

Height ___ ft. ___ Weight _____ Hair _____ Eyes _____

Complexion _____ Bust _____ Waist _____ Thigh _____

Neck _____ Hat _____ Shoes _____ Teeth _____

Marks on body _____

Appendix D

Villa's Forces at Columbus, New Mexico
March 9, 1916[1]

ADVANCE GUARD
Colonel Candelario Cervantes   80 men

MAIN BODY
Colonel Nicolas Hernandez   60 men

General Villa, Headquarters
    Staff and Escort   80 men

General Pablo Lopez   100 men

General Juan Pedrosa   40 men

General Francisco Beltran   125 men

"The rear guard consisted of ten men belonging to Beltran's detachment. Altogether there were 485 men in the attacking party."[2]

---

[1] James A. Sandos, "German Involvement in Northern Mexico, 1915-1916: A New Look at the Columbus Raid," *Hispanic American Historical Review* L:1 (February 1970), 77.

[2] *Ibid.* Sandos' figures are taken from the Pershing Papers, Box 372.

Appendix E

Statement for the press:
Washington, March 10, 1916.

There is no intention of entering Mexico in force. A sufficient body of mobile troops will be sent in to locate and disperse or capture the band or bands that attacked Columbus. As soon as the de facto government can take control of the situation, any forces of the United States then remaining in Mexico will of course be withdrawn.[1]

Washington. March 10th, 1916
MEMORANDUM FOR THE ADJUTANT GENERAL:[2]

The Secretary of War directs that the following telegram be coded without delay and sent to the Commanding General, Southern Department:

You will promptly organize an adequate military force under the command of Brigadier General J. J. Pershing and will direct him to proceed promptly across the border in pursuit of the Mexican band which attacked the town of Columbus and the troops there on the morning of the 9th instant. These troops will be withdrawn to American territory as soon as the de facto Government of Mexico is able to relieve them of this work. In any event the work of these troops will be regarded as finished as soon as Villa's band or bands are known to be broken up. In carrying out these instructions you are authorized to employ whatever guides and interpreters are necessary and you are given general authority to employ such transportation, including motor transportation, with necessary civilian personnel as may be required. The President his following instructions to be carefully adhered to and to be kept strictly confidential. You will instruct the commanders of your troops on the border opposite the states of Chihuahua and Sonora, or, roughly, within the field of possible operations by Villa and not under the control of the forces of the de facto government, that they are authorized to use the same tactics of defense and pursuit in the event of similar raids across the border and into the Unites States by a band or bands such as attacked Columbus yesterday. You are instructed to make all practicable use of the aeroplanes at San Antonio for observation. Telegraph for whatever reinforcements or material you need. Notify this office as to force selected and expedite movement.

H. L. Scott[3]

A PRESS RELEASE
March 10, 1916

An adequate force will be sent at once in pursuit of Villa with the single object of capturing him and putting a stop to his forays. This can and will be done in entirely friendly aid of the constituted authorities in Mexico and with scrupulous respect for the sovereignty of that Republic.*

*This press release was issued immediately after the cabinet meeting on March 10 as an official statement from the White House.[4]

Pershing's First General Order
March 14, 1916

II. (2) "... the only purpose of this expedition is to assist in apprehending and capturing Villa and his bandits."[5]

Clarence C. Clendenen, "The Punitive Expedition of 1916: A Re-Evaluation," *Arizona and the West* 3:4 (Winter 1961), 311-20, offers an assessment of the expedition from the perspective of an Army cavalry officer.

---

[1] *Papers of Woodrow Wilson,* Vol. 36, 284-85.
[2] Henry Pinckney McCain, Brigadier General, U.S.A.
[3] *PWW*, Vol. 36, 285-86.
[4] *Ibid.,* 287.
[5] Herbert M. Mason, *The Great Pursuit* (New York: Random House, 1970), Appendix B, 245.

Appendix F

Prisoners From Pancho Villa's Raid
at Columbus, New Mexico
March 9, 1916[1]

Number	Name	Age	Occupation
554 CJ	Alvares, Francisco	22	Laborer
556 CJ	Castillo, Juan	26	Laborer
552 CJ	Garcia, Taurino	21	Laborer
555 CJ	Rangel, José	23	Laborer
551 CJ	Renteria, Eusevio	24	Laborer
553 CJ	Rodriguez, José	20	Laborer
550 CJ	Sanchez, Juan	16	Laborer

---

[1]*New Mexico Federal Prisoner Roster 1913 - 1952.* State Records Center and Archives, Santa Fe, New Mexico. Francisco Alvares and Juan Sanchez were hanged June 9, 1916. Juan Castillo, Taurino Garcia, Jose Rangel, and Eusevio Renteria were hanged June 30, 1916.

In a later interview with Governor McDonald, Garcia stated he was a tailor by trade and had worked in shops in Oaxaca and Mexico City. Silver City *Independent,* July 4. 1916

Appendix G

Prisoners From Pancho Villa's Raid
at Columbus, New Mexico
March 9, 1916

Number	Name	Age	Occupation
4071	Borciaga[o], Pedro*	24	Laborer
4067	Bustamente, Rafael*	22	Laborer
4066	Bustillos, Ramon	18	Laborer
4069	Camareno, Tomas	47	Farmer
4074	Gutierrez, Lorenzo	33	Laborer
4078	Jimenez, Mariano	21	Mechanic
4076	Lopez, Pedro	21	Baker
4073	Marquez, José de la Luz	23	Laborer
4079	Muñoz, Juan*	25	Farmer
4080	Rodriguez, David*	23	Laborer
4075	Rodriguez, Rafael	44	Laborer
4081	Salis, Francisco*	29	Laborer
4072	Tena, José	23	Laborer
4082	Torres, Juan	25	Laborer
4070	Torres, Santos	21	Laborer
4077	Vargas, Silvino*	18	Laborer

*These men were brought back by the Pershing expedition. Each prisoner was tried for murder in Luna County, 6th Judicial District Court,

Judge R.R. Ryan presiding. All were citizens of Mexico; all pleaded guilty to second-degree murder; all were sentenced to seventy to eighty years in the Penitentiary. Terms commenced August 27, 1917; they were received at the Penitentiary in Santa Fe August 28, 1917.

The youngest was 18; the oldest was 47; the average age was 25.

---

[1]*Penitentiary Record Book of Convicts, November 2, 1884 - September 27, 1917*. State Records Center and Archives Santa Fe, New Mexico.
* These men were identified as Lieutenants by the *Deming Headlight*, History File #26, SRCCA.

Appendix H

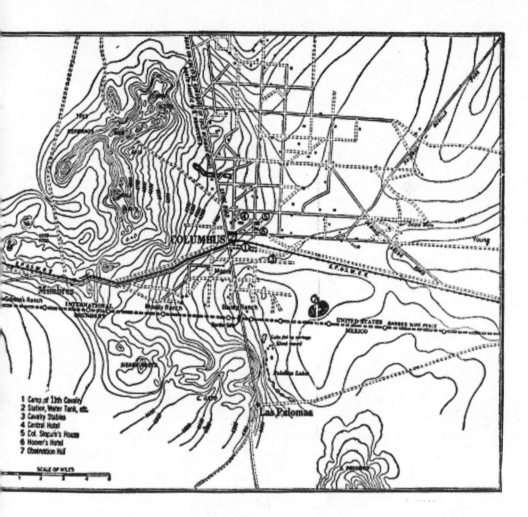

Columbus, New Mexico, and surrounding area
at the time of Villa's raid.
(from Review of Reviews, April 1916)

Appendix I

Prisoners taken by the Punitive Expedition[1]

Celso Apodaca	Juan Meza
Pedro Borciaga	Juan B. Muñoz
Raphael Bustamante	David Rodríguez
Ramón Bustillos	José Rodríguez
Tomás Camarena	Raphael Rodríguez
Francisco Heras	Francisco Solís
Manuel C. Jiménez	José Tena
Mariano Jimenez	Juan Torres
Pedro López	Juan R. Torres
José de la Luz Marquez	Santos Torres
José Meza	Silvino Vargas

According to Alberto Calzadíaz Barrera, prisoners Francisco Heras (Namiquipa, Chihuahua), Pedro López (Mexico City), José Meza (Cumpas, Sonora), and Juan R. Torres (Zacatecas) died of malnutrition and abuse while in the jail at Silver City, New Mexico.[2] Francisco Heras (or Herras) was indicted with the "Columbus 19", but there is no record of imprisonment in the New Mexico State Penitentiary (NMSP). Pedro López was prisoner #4076 (NMSP) and on April 30, 1921 returned to Mexico a free man. There is no record of either the indictment or the imprisonment of Juan Meza (or Mesa) and Juan R. Torres. There is no indictment record for Celso Apodaca, Manual C. Jiménez or José Meza. An examination of the Grant County Death Records, 1873-1987, revealed no death records for Francisco Heras (or Herras), Juan Meza (or Mesa) or Juan R Torres.[3]

In the course of the present writer's research, the only reference claiming deliberate abuse of Villista prisoners has been Calzadíaz Berrera.[4] No mention of death as a result of deliberate abuse has been found in court records, jail records, prison records, newspaper accounts, political memoirs, private journals, or diaries. In reporting the transfer of seventeen Villistas from Silver City to

100

the State Penitentiary, the Santa Fe *New Mexican* stated,

> They had been kept in jail in Silver City because of the
> lack of accommodation of the Luna county jail at
> Deming. Three other Mexican bandits had been cap-
> tured by the American troops. One of them died in
> prison, a second is sick at Silver City, and a third es-
> caped from escort back into Mexico. Guadalupe Chavez,
> also charged with participation in the massacre, pleaded
> not guilty and will be tried at the fall term of court."[5]

The nature of the abuse, as related to Calzadíaz Berrera by
Juan B. Muñoz, was that the prisoners were kept in the basement
of the Silver City jail and were fed only twice a day. The morning
meal consisted of black bread and oats and one-half cup of coffee
without sugar; the evening meal consisted of black bread, a plate
of beans ("... *un plato con cuarenta granitos de frijo l...*"), and coffee
without sugar. The diet remained the same day after day, and
according to Muñoz, the result was the death of four of the Villistas.[6]

---

[1] Alberto Calzadíaz Barrera, *Por Que Villa ataco Columbus: Intriga internacional* (Mexico, D. F.: Editores Mexicanos Unidos, 1972), 113-14.

[2] *Ibid.*, 114. Friedrich Katz claims "...sadistic guards gave them [the prisoners] so little food that two of their number died of malnutriton...". Katz, *The Life & Times of Pancho Villa*, 608. Curiously, Katz's source is Calzadiaz Berrera.

[3] Grant County Death Records, 1873-1987, Public Library, Silver City, New Mexico.

[4] He also reports that the prisoners arrived in Silver City on June 28, 1916, yet neither Silver City newspaper, the *Independent* nor the *Enterprise*, makes mention of the arrival of the Villistas.

[5] "17 More Villista Bandits Arrive At State Prison To Make Long Visit," Santa Fe *New Mexican*, August 28, 1917, 3.

[6] Calzadíaz Berrera, *op. cit.*, 114.

Appendix J

Record of Mexican Prisoners in Confinement at the Stockade
Colonia Dublan, Mexico
July 4, 1916[1]

Name	Unit[2]	Home
1. Adame, Enrique[3] (Pvt.)	Col. Fernandez	San Geronimo Ranch
2. Borciaga, Pedro (Lt.)	Cervantes' Bodyguard	Namiquipa
3. Bustillos, Ramon (Pvt.)	Cervantes	Namiquipa
4. Camarena, Tomas (Pvt.)	Cervantes	Cruces
5. Chavez, Guadalupe (Pvt.)	Cervantes	Namiquipa
6. Gomez, Pilar (Civilian)	————	El Carmen Ranch[4]
7. Gutierrez, Lorenzo (Cpl.)	Pedrosa	San Andres
8. Herras, Francisco (Pvt.)	Hernadez	Namiquipa
9. Jimenez, Mariano (Lt.)	Villa's escort	San Luiz Patosi
10. Lopez, Pedro (Pvt.)	Hernandez	Mexico City
11. Lujan, Pedro (Lt. Col.)[5]	Cervantes	Namiquipa
12. Marquez, José de la Luz (Pvt.)	Fernandez	Rancho Rivera
13. Mejia, Francisco (Lt.)	Hernandez	Jaliosco State
14. Mesa, Juan (Pvt.)	Beltran	Sonora
15. Muñoz, Juan (Lt.)	Cervantes	Namiquipa
16. Tena, José (Pvt.)	Suarez	Namiquipa
17. Rodriguez, David (Lt.)	Cervantes	Ocampo
18. Rodriguez, Raphael (Pvt.)	Hernandez	Namiquipa
19. Solis, Francisco (Lt.)	Cervantes	Namiquipa
20. Torres, Juan (Lt.)	Cervantes	Namiquipa
21. Torres, Santos (Lt.)	Cervantes	Namiquipa
22. Vargas, Silvino (Lt.)	Cervantes	Cruces

All of the above listed prisoners admitted the charge of participation in the attack on Columbus, New Mexico on June 9, 1916, with the exception of Pilar Gomez and Pedro Lujan. Both men were released.

In addition to the twenty-two recorded above, Victor Ceja Reyes lists Manuel Bustillos, Celso Apodaca, Rafael Bustamante, Manuel C. Jimémez, David Rodríguez, José Rodríguez, J. Carmen Ortíz, Lorenzo Rodríguez, Florencio Varela, Refugio Licano, and Guadalupe Chávez.[6]

[1] National Archives, Record Group 395, Headquarters Historical Data Intelligence Files, Punitive Expedition to Mexico Headquarters, 1916-17, "Record of Prisoners" Box 1, E-1210.

[2] The unit of command under which the accused Villista had served in the raid on Columbus, March 9, 1916.

[3] Adame's claim to have been forced from the line of march near Ojitos before reaching Columbus due to illness was corroborated by two other Villistas (Borciago and Marquez). He rejoined Villa's forces March 15, 1916 near Corralitos.

[4] Accused of wire cutting, confined June 16, 1916, later released.

[5] Accused of recruiting men for the raid on Columbus, admitted the charge, later released.

[6] Victor Ceja Reyes, *Yo, Francisco Villa y Columbus* (Centro Librero la Prensa, S.A de C.V., 1987), 218.

Appendix K[1]

Villista Casualties at Columbus, March 9, 1916

OFFICERS

Colonel Enriquez	Killed
Lt. Colonel Pablo Sanchez	Killed
Lt. Colonel Cruz Chavez	Killed
Lt. Colonel Carmen Ortiz	Killed
Lt. Colonel Cipriano Vargas	Killed
Major Pablo Vasquez	Killed
Major Pablo Chavez	Killed
Major Trinidad Castillo	Killed
Major Jesus Baeza	Killed
Captain Francisco Antonio Perez	Killed
Captain Julian Aguirre	Killed
Captain Francisco	Killed
Captain José Gonzales	Wounded
Captain Arcadio Baldanio	Wounded

ALL RANKS

Ninety killed (included those who died of their wounds)

Twenty-three wounded

Further Casualties Reported by the Punitive Expedition

Of the four hundred and eighty-five Villistas who attacked Columbus, New Mexico March 9, 1916, two hundred and seventy-three were reported killed, one hundred and eight were wounded who were not captured. Nineteen were held in confinement, one hundred and fifty-six were still at large (of whom sixty were amnestied by the *de facto* government), and thirty-seven were unaccounted for.[2]

---

[1] John J. Pershing, "Punitive Expedition Report," (Colonia Dublan, Mexico, October 10, 1916), U.S. Army Military History Institute, Carlisle Barracks, Pa., 96.

[2] *Ibid.*, 97.

Appendix L

Itinerary of Francisco Villa, March 8 to June 30, 1916[1]

"From information obtained through native sources after very careful inquiry by the officers of the Intelligence Department of the Expedition, the following facts have been compiled regarding the attack on Columbus, March 9, 1916, and the flight of Villa thereafter:"

"At daylight the Villistas could see that the number of American soldiers greatly exceeded the number that had been reported to them. Their retreat commenced at 6:30 o'clock a.m., by men carrying away the wounded to the rear where their reserve and mounts were located; these were followed by individual skirmishers and then by groups. The threats of Villa who had remained with the horses through the action were insufficient to stop them and return [them] to the fight. At 7:15 o'clock a.m., practically the entire Villa force except Cervantes and Fernandez and a small detachment had retreated. The leaders were charged with their own wounded, and as these arrived from the town they were strapped and tied to their mounts. Cervantes joined at about 7:30 o'clock a.m., when the retreat of the Villistas into Mexico began in earnest, but with great confusion. Villa, in person, with an escort of about thirty men occupied a ridge about three miles southeast of Columbus in order to cover the retreat of groups that had been delayed. The retreat was continued to the north bank of the Bocas Grandes River at a point about one mile west of Vade de Fusiles, which was reached at about 1:00 p.m. Orders for a halt were here given ... and an effort was made to check the losses. Villa, in person, made the check assisted by Manuel Baca and Ramon Tarango; he there announced that about one hundred men were unaccounted for as killed, wounded or missing."

---

[1] John J. Pershing, "Punitive Expedition Report," (Colonia Dublan, Mexico, October 10, 1916), U.S. Army Military History Institute, Carlisle Barracks, PA, Appendix N, 98; 99-100.

Appendix M

The question of insurance arose at Senator Albert B. Fall's Senate Subcommittee on Foreign Relations hearings in El Paso on February 7, 1920. Among the witnesses was Mrs. Laura Ritchie of Columbus, New Mexico whose husband had been proprietor of the Commercial Hotel at the time of Villa's raid. Mr. Ritchie was killed during the raid, and the Commercial Hotel caught fire. Mrs. Ritchie testified that "...we saw them putting oil on the Lemon & Payne store, and then we could see, I guess, thousands of Mexicans out there by the light of the fire, and our hotel caught fire, and I do not think they set fire to it, but it caught fire ... ."[1] Her testimony continued:

Senator Fall: "Mrs. Ritchie, did you or your husband own that property, the Commercial Hotel?"

Mrs. Ritchie: "No, sir; my husband built the hotel for Sam Ravel, and we rented it and the furniture and everything was mine."

Senator Fall: "Did you have any other property than the furnishings of the hotel?"

Mrs. Ritchie: "Yes, sir; the building back of the hotel, just a little small building."

Senator Fall: "Have you ever received any remuneration or recompense from any source whatsoever for your loses at Columbus?"

Mrs. Ritchie: No, sir; not even any insurance."

Senator Fall: Did you have the building or furniture insured?

Mrs. Ritchie: "Yes, sir."

Senator Fall: "And you have received no insurance for its destruction?"

Mrs. Ritchie: "Not a penny."

Senator Fall: "What was the reason, do you know?"

Mrs. Ritchie: "They called it an invasion."[2]

She went on to explain to Senator Fall that her insurance policy had a clause which excluded damage caused by an invasion into the United States. The company refused to accept responsibility or to pay for any loses, which meant that the Ritchies had literally lost everything. Senator Fall asked Mrs. Ritchie to send the name and address of the insurance company to his committee, implying that he would look into the matter.[3]

[1] U.S. Congress, Senate, Subcommittee of the Committee on Foreign Relations, *Investigation of Mexican Affairs.* [66th Congress, 2nd Session, Senate Documents, Vol. IX, 1919-1929, #7665] Washington: Government Printing Office, 1921, 1621-22.

[2] *Ibid.,* 1604-05.

[3] *Ibid.,* 1605. The present writer has found no documentation indicating that Mrs. Ritchie was compensated for losses by her insurance company.

A Brief Note On Sources

The sources used are to be found in the footnotes and, to a lesser extent, in the text itself. The trial transcript, Renteria *et als*[1], was indispensable to the narrative. The papers of Governors McDonald, Larrazolo, and Mecham provided invaluable information, as did the pages of the Santa Fe *New Mexican*. The microfilm of the *New Mexico Territorial Penitentiary Roster, 1884-1917*, and the *New Mexico Federal Prisoner Roster, 1913-1952* proved helpful in learning more about the Villistas. The microfiche copies of criminal records in the Luna County Clerk's Office, Deming, New Mexico, provided forty indictments of alleged Villistas and were a source of miscellaneous other documents of value. The papers of President Woodrow Wilson (*PPW*) contain correspondence which provide insight into the interest his administration had in the fate of the Villistas, as well as conveying Washington's concern over possible international repercussions the trials might have had. Senator Fall's Senate Subcommittee hearings provide a great deal of helpful testimony from citizens of Columbus who were present during the raid. The Charles Poe Family Photo Collection and the New Mexico Department of Corrections Photograph Collection, both at the State Records Center and Archives, Santa Fe, are invaluable sources. At the National Archives in Washington, DC, Record Group 395, World War I Organizational Records, Headquarters Historical Data 11.4, Intelligence Files, Records of Prisoners, provided much necessary information on those Villistas who were brought back to the United States by the Punitive Expedition.

Suggested Readings

As the introductory pages of this essay demonstrate, the reader of published material about Francisco Villa and the raid on Columbus must follow the old adage: *caveat lector*. Much has been published based on secondary and even tertiary sources, with all the weaknesses and errors of such sources sometimes magnified.

---

[1] *Cf.* Page 6, fn. 25.

The following secondary sources and scholarly articles should provide the reader with a solid foundation upon which to begin his or her journey into the fascinating world of our century's beginnings: a transition from the relative peace and stability of the nineteenth century into the turmoil of war and revolution which has been so much a part of the twentieth century.

Books

Braady, Haldeen. *Pancho Villa At Columbus: The Raid of 1916*. Southwestern Studies, III:1 (Spring 1965). Texas Western College, 1965.

_____. *Pershing's Mission in Mexico*. El Paso, Texas: Texas Western Press, 1966.

_____. *The Paradox of Pancho Villa*. El Paso, Texas: Texas Western Press, 1978.

Calzadia Barrera, Alberto. *Por Que Villa ataco Columbus: Intriga Internacional*. Mexico, D. F.: Editores Mexicanos Unidos, 1972.

Cervantes, Frederico M. *Francisco Villa y la Revolución*. Mexico, D.F.: Ediciones Alonso, 1960.

Clendenen, Clarence C. *Blood on the Border*. New York: Macmillan and Co., 1969.

_____. *The United States and Pancho Villa: A Study in Unconventional Diplomacy*. Ithaca, New York: Cornel University Press, 1961.

Finnegan, John P. *Military Intelligence*. Washington, DC: Center of Military History, U.S. Army, 1998.

Friedman, Leon. *The Law of War: A Documentary History*. New York: Random House, Inc., 1972.

Eisenhower, John S. D. *Intervention! The United States and the Mexican Revolution, 1913-1917*. New York: Random House, 1970.

Harris, Larry A. *Pancho Villa: Strong Man of the Revolution*. Silver City, New Mexico: High-Lonesome Books, 1995.

Harris, Charles H. and Louis R. Sadler. *The Border and the Revolution: Clandestine Activities of the Mexican Revolution: 1910-1920*. Silver City, New Mexico: High-Lonesome Books, 1988.

Katz, Friedrich. *The Life & Times of Pancho Villa*. Stanford, California: Stanford University Press, 1998.

_____. *The Secret War in Mexico: Europe, the United States and the Mexican Revolution*. Chicago and London: University of Chicago Press, 1981.

Krause, Enrique. *Mexico, Biography of Power: A History of Modern Mexico, 1819-1996*. New York: Harper Perennial, 1998.

Link, Arthur S, ed. *The Papers of Woodrow Wilson*. Princeton, NJ: Princeton University Press, 1981.

Mason, Herbert M. *The Great Pursuit*. New York: Random House, 1970.

Reyes, Victor Ceja. *Yo, Francisco Villa y Columbus*. Centro Librero la Prensa, S.S. de C.V., 1987.

Tomkins, Frank (Col.). *Chasing Villa: The Last Campaign of the U.S. Cavalry*. Silver City, New Mexico: High-Lonesome Books, 1996.

Articles

Clendenen, Clarence C. "The Punitive Expedition of 1916: A Re-Evaluation," *Arizona and the West* 3:4 (Winter 1961), 311-20.

Hall, Linda B. and Don M. Coerver. "Woodrow Wilson, Public Opinion, and the Punitive Expedition: A Re-Assessment," *New Mexico Historical Review* 72:2 (April 1997), 171-94.

Katz, Friedrich. "Pancho Villa and the Attack on Columbus, New Mexico," *The American Historical Review* 83:1 (February 1978), 101-30.

_____. "Pancho Villa," *Essays On the Mexican Revolution: Revisionist Views of the Leaders,* George Wolfskill and Douglas W. Richmond, (Eds.) Austin and London: University of Texas Press, 1979.

Mahoney, Tom. "The Columbus Raid," *Southwest Review* 17:2 (January 1932), 161-71.

McGaw, Bill. "Was Pancho Villa Paid $80,000 For Making the Raid On Columbus?," *The Southwesterner* 3:11 (May 1964).

Munch, Francis J. "Villa's Columbus Raid: Practical Politics or German Design," *New Mexico Historical Review* 40:3 (July 1969), 189-214.

Naylor, Thomas H. "Massacre At San Pedro de la Cueva: The Significance of Pancho Villa's Disastrous Sonora Campaign," *The Western Historical Quarterly* VIII:2 (April 1977), 124-50.

Osorio, Rubén. "*Villismo:* Nationalism and Popular Mobilization in Northern Mexico," in *Rural Revolt in Mexico: U. S. Intervention and the Domain of Subaltern Politics,* ed. Daniel Nugent (Durhan & London: Duke University Press, 1998).

Pilcher, Jeffrey M. "Pancho Villa Rides Into Mexican Legend Or, The Cavalry Myth and Military Tactics in the Mexican Revolution," *Military History of the West* 26:1 (Spring 1996), 1-22

Sandos, James A. "German Involvement In Northern Mexico, 1915-1916: A New Look At the Columbus Raid," *Hispanic American Historical Review* L:1 (February 1970), 70-88.

Tate, Michael L. "Pershing's Punitive Expedition: Pursuer of Bandits or Presidential Panacea," *The Americas* 32:1 (July 1975), 46-71.

Tobler, Hans Werner. "Peasants and the Revolutionary State," in *Riot, Rebellion, and Revolution: Rural Social Conflict in Mexico,* ed. Friedrich Katz (Princeton, NJ: Princeton University Press, 1988).

White, E. Bruce. "The Muddied Waters of Columbus New Mexico," *The Americas* 32:1 (July 1975), 72-98.

Wolff, Leon. "Black Jack's Mexican Goose Chase," *American Heritage* XIII:4 (June 1962), 22-27; 100-06.

Yockelson, Mitchell. "The United States Armed Forces and the Mexican Punitive Expedition," Part I, *Prologue* 29:3 (Fall 1997).

Young, Karl. "A Fight That Could Have Meant War," *The American West* III:2 (Spring 1966), 16-23; 90.

Miscellaneous

Johnson, R. B. "The Punitive Expedition: A Military, Diplomatic, and Political History of Pershing's Chase After Pancho Villa", Unpublished PhD Dissertation, University of Southern California, 1964.

"John J. Pershing: A Selected Bibliography of MHI Sources," United States Army Military History Institute, Reference Branch, August 1989, August 1994.

"Mexican Revolution, 1911-1921: A Working Bibliography of MHI Sources," United States Army Military History Institute, Reference Branch, October 1988.

"Mexican Border, 1911-21: A Working Bibliography of MHI Sources," United States Army Military History Institute, Reference Branch, October 1988, March 1992, November 1994.

"Mexican Punitive Expedition, 1916-17: A Bibliography of MHI Sources," United States Military History Institute, Reference Branch, July 1989, March 1992, November 1994.

Monticone, Joseph R., "Revolutionary Mexico and the U.S. Southwest: The Columbus Raid." Unpublished M.A. thesis, California State University, Fullerton, 1981.

Pershing, John J. "Punitive Expedition Report," Colonia Dublan, Mexico, October 10, 1916 (Army War College: Carlisle Barracks, PA).

INDEX

James W. Hurst is Professor Emeritus of History, Joliet (Illinois) Junior College. A native of Illinois he attended Southern Illinois University at Carbondale. After an active teaching career at secondary and college levels, he and his wife moved to New Mexico and currently live in Mesilla. Since arriving in New Mexico, Hurst has become interested in the history of this area and *The Villista Prisoners of 1916-17* is a result of that interest.